ARE YOU READY

AND AS IT IS APPOINTED UNTO MEN ONCE
TO DIE, BUT AFTER THIS THE JUDGMENT:
HEBREWS 9:27

LEO R. LAVINKA

Copyright © 2018 by Leo R. LaVinka
All Rights Reserved
Printed in the United States of America
August 21, 2018

REL067030: Religion: Christian Theology – Apologetics.

ISBN 978-1-7321746-0-3

All Scripture quotes are from the King James Bible.

No part of this work may be reproduced without the expressed consent of the publisher, except for brief quotes, whether by electronic, photocopying, recording, or information storage and retrieval systems.

[Publisher's Note: The author used all caps in this work to emphasize the importance of the words.]

Address All Inquiries To:
THE OLD PATHS PUBLICATIONS, Inc.
142 Gold Flume Way
Cleveland, Georgia, U.S.A. 30528

Web: www.theoldpathspublications.com
E-mail: TOP@theoldpathspublications.com

DEDICATION

I DEDICATE THIS BOOK TO MY WIFE, ELSIE, MY CHILDREN, GRANDCHILDREN, GREAT GRANDCHILDREN, AND ALL THEIR FAMILIES. MY PRAYER IS THAT IT WILL BE READ, ACCEPTED, AND APPLIED TO THEIR LIVES.

                              LEO R. LAVINKA

ARE YOU READY?

FOREWORD

THIS DISPENSATION OF GRACE IS APPARENTLY FAST APPROACHING ITS END. WE ARE DRIFTING FURTHER AND FURTHER AWAY FROM GOD'S TRUTH WHICH IS REVEALED IN HIS HOLY WORD. IN OUR OWN COUNTRY CHRISTIANS ARE ON A GOVERNMENT WATCH LIST AND ARE BEING DISCRIMINATED AGAINST FOR THEIR BELIEFS. OUR HOLY BIBLE (KJV) IS BEING DILUTED AND PRINTED IN MANY (SO CALLED) MORE ACCURATE TRANSLATIONS. MANY PREACHERS HAVE FALLEN INTO SATAN'S TRAP OF SEEKING LARGE NUMBERS RATHER THAN PREACHING THE ENTIRE WORD OF GOD. AS A RESULT, I AM AFRAID THAT MANY PEOPLE HAVE A HEAD KNOWLEDGE OF CHRIST (LOST), BUT NOT A HEART KNOWLEDGE (SAVED). MANY CHRISTIANS TODAY ARE SATISFIED IN KNOWING THEY ARE SAVED AND ARE GOING ABOUT THEIR SELF-SERVING BUSINESS WITH VERY LITTLE DESIRE TO REALLY SERVE GOD OUT OF PURE LOVE FOR HIM. I AM PERSONALLY CONVICTED OF MY OWN SHORT COMINGS. THIS BOOK SELECTS SIX TOPICS OF SCRIPTURE WHICH I BELIEVE WILL ENCOURAGE THOSE WHO READ IT TO SEARCH THE SCRIPTURES FOR ASSURANCE OF THEIR SALVATION AND WHAT GOD EXPECTS FROM HIS CHURCH, THE BODY OF BELIEVERS.

ARE YOU READY?

TABLE OF CONTENTS

DEDICATION 3
FOREWORD 5
TABLE OF CONTENTS 7
INTRODUCTION 9
CHAPTER 1: THE JUDGMENT SEAT OF CHRIST 11
CHAPTER 2: GREAT WHITE THRONE JUDGMENT .. 37
CHAPTER 3: HELL 67
   WHEN WAS HELL CREATED? 72
   WHERE IS HELL? 74
   HOW LONG WILL THE LOST BE IN HELL AND WHAT IS THE PUNISHMENT? 78
   ARE THERE DIFFERENT DEGREES OF PUNISHMENT IN HELL? 81
CHAPTER 4: HEAVEN 97
CHAPTER 5: JESUS CHRIST 109
CHAPTER 6: SIN AND SALVATION 129
INDEX 147
SCRIPTURE REFERENCES 175
ABOUT THE AUTHOR 185

ARE YOU READY?

INTRODUCTION

AS I GET CLOSER TO MY HOMEGOING TO BE WITH MY LORD AND SAVIOUR JESUS CHRIST, I HAVE BECOME MORE KEENLY AWARE THAT I WILL BE JUDGED AT THE JUDGMENT SEAT OF CHRIST. I KNOW MY SINS (AS A CHRISTIAN) ARE FORGIVEN AND REMEMBERED NO MORE, AND THE DOORS OF HEAVEN WILL BE OPEN, BUT I WILL BE JUDGED FOR BOTH MY GOOD AND BAD. HOW MANY (OR HOW FEW) WILL HEAR THE WORDS "WELL DONE THOU GOOD AND FAITHFUL SERVANT"? WHAT GOOD HAVE I ACCOMPLISHED AND WHAT IS MY BAD IN GOD'S JUDGMENT, NOT MINE? THIS QUESTION TO ME IS A SOBERING REALITY! I AM FULLY AWARE THAT OUR SERVICE TO GOD (AFTER WE ARE SAVED) IS TO BE ACCOMPLISHED OUT OF A PURE LOVE FOR HIM BECAUSE HE FIRST LOVED US. *"IF YOU LOVE ME, KEEP MY COMMANDMENTS."* (JOHN 14:15); *"IF A MAN LOVE ME, HE WILL KEEP MY WORDS."* (JOHN 14:23b); *HE THAT LOVETH ME NOT KEEPETH NOT MY SAYINGS."* (JOHN 14:24a).

I ALSO WANT MY CHILDREN, GRANDCHILDREN, AND GREAT GRAND-CHILDREN (SHOULD JESUS TARRY) TO HAVE A KNOWLEDGE AS TO WHAT I BELIEVE TO BE MOST IMPORTANT, AND TO HELP CREATE IN THEM A DESIRE TO STUDY ALL SCRIPTURE. THIS BOOK WAS ORIGINALLY JUST MY

THOUGHTS DEVELOPED FOR THAT PURPOSE. I SHARED THEM WITH MY FRIEND, DR. H.D. WILLIAMS, WHO ENCOURAGED ME TO PUT THEM IN BOOK FORM FOR OTHERS TO READ. MY PRAYER IS THAT ALL WHO READ IT WILL BENEFIT.

THESE COMMENTS ARE THE RESULT OF YEARS OF LEARNING FROM MANY GREAT PREACHERS, READING SOME GREAT BOOKS AND COMMENTARIES, SEARCHING MY NOTES AND TEACHING LESSONS OVER THE LAST HALF CENTURY, AND MY PERSONAL STUDY AND LIMITED BIBLE KNOWLEDGE. I CAN'T THANK OTHERS ENOUGH FOR HAVING THE OPPORTUNITY TO LEARN FROM THEM.

I VERY MUCH APPRECIATE THE HELP OF MY WIFE, ELSIE, AND DR. AND MRS. H.D. WILLIAMS FOR THEIR VALUABLE ADVICE AND ASSISTANCE IN FINALIZING THIS PROJECT. TO GOD BE THE GLORY!

CHAPTER 1
THE JUDGMENT SEAT OF CHRIST

PSALM 11:5. THE WORD JUDGMENT OR ITS DERIVATIVES ARE LISTED SEVERAL HUNDRED TIMES IN THE BIBLE (758+ TIMES). GOD HATES SIN!! THERE IS COMING A DAY WHEN HE WILL JUDGE WITH RIGHTEOUSNESS, TRUTH, AND JUSTICE. ARE YOU READY?

> *Psalm 11:5 The LORD trieth the righteous: but the wicked and him that loveth violence his soul hateth.*

PROVERBS 1:31, ISAIAH 53:6, EZEKIEL 22:31, MATTHEW 7:21-23. WE ALL TEND TO DO WHAT WE CONSIDER, OR THINK IS RIGHT IN OUR OWN EYES. GOD CALLS THAT INIQUITY. THINK ABOUT THAT.

> *Proverbs 1:31 Therefore shall they eat of the fruit of their own way, and be filled with their own devices.*
>
> *Isaiah 53:6 All we like sheep have gone astray; we have turned every one to his own way; and the LORD hath laid on him the iniquity of us all.*
>
> *Ezekiel 22:31 Therefore have I poured out mine indignation upon them; I have consumed them with the fire of my wrath: their own way have*

I recompensed upon their heads, saith the Lord GOD.

***Matthew 7:21-23** Not every one that saith unto me, Lord, Lord, shall enter into the kingdom of heaven; but he that doeth the will of my Father which is in heaven. **22** Many will say to me in that day, Lord, Lord, have we not prophesied in thy name? and in thy name have cast out devils? and in thy name done many wonderful works? **23** And then will I profess unto them, I never knew you: depart from me, ye that work iniquity.*

2 CORINTHIANS 5:10, MATTHEW 25:41, 46. ONLY BORN AGAIN <u>CHRISTIANS WILL BE JUDGED AT THE JUDGMENT SEAT OF CHRIST</u>. THE <u>LOST WILL BE JUDGED AT THE GREAT WHITE THRONE JUDGMENT</u> WHERE THEY WILL RECEIVE EVERLASTING TORMENT AND BE ETERNALLY SEPARATED FROM GOD.

***2 Corinthians 5:10** For we must all appear before the judgment seat of Christ; that every one may receive the things done in his body, according to that he hath done, whether it be good or bad.*

***Matthew 25:41** Then shall he say also unto them on the left hand, Depart from me, ye cursed, into*

CHAPTER 1: THE JUDGMENT SEAT OF CHRIST

everlasting fire, prepared for the devil and his angels:

Matthew 25:46 *And these shall go away into everlasting punishment: but the righteous into life eternal.*

TODAY I WANT YOU TO CONSIDER WHAT THE JUDGMENT SEAT OF CHRIST WILL BE LIKE.

CERTAINLY, CHRIST'S HOLINESS WILL BE VINDICATED. HE IS GOD! HE WILL JUDGE BOTH THE GOOD AND BAD THINGS WHICH WE HAVE DONE. I KNOW FOR THE GOOD WE MAY RECEIVE REWARDS, BUT WHAT ABOUT THE "BAD"? WE KNOW OUR SINS ARE FORGIVEN. SO, WHAT IS THE "BAD"? IN THE GREEK, "BAD" MEANS WICKED, VICIOUS, BAD IN CONDUCT AND IN CHARACTER. IT CAN ALSO MEAN "IMPOSTER, OR A "PRETENDER."

GOD IS PERFECTION PERSONIFIED. HE <u>WILL</u> JUDGE BY <u>HIS</u> DEFINITION OF "BAD," NOT OURS.

I BELIEVE WHEN I AM JUDGED I WILL SEE CLEARLY ALL THE "BAD" WHICH I HAVE DONE. I BELIEVE I'LL BE ASHAMED TO LOOK UPON MY GOD WHO PAID SUCH A HIGH PRICE FOR MY SALVATION. TO ME, THIS IS A FRIGHTENING THOUGHT.

1 CORINTHIANS 3:11-15, JOHN 12:47. OUR SINS ARE FORGIVEN, BUT OUR <u>WORKS</u> WILL BE TRIED. THERE IS ONLY ONE

FOUNDATION THAT OUR <u>WORKS</u> (OR DEEDS) CAN BUILD UPON. THAT IS <u>JESUS CHRIST AND HIS WORDS</u>.

***1 Corinthians 3:11** For other foundation can no man lay than that is laid, which is Jesus Christ. **12** Now if any man build upon this foundation gold, silver, precious stones, wood, hay, stubble; **13** Every man's work shall be made manifest: for the day shall declare it, because it shall be revealed by fire; and the fire shall try every man's work of what sort it is. **14** If any man's work abide which he hath built thereupon, he shall receive a reward. **15** If any man's work shall be burned, he shall suffer loss: but he himself shall be saved; yet so as by fire.*

***John 12:47** And if any man hear my words, and believe not, I judge him not: for I came not to judge the world, but to save the world. **48** He that rejecteth me, and receiveth not my words, hath one that judgeth him: the word that I have spoken, the same shall judge him in the last day.*

EVERY MAN'S WORKS SHALL BE MADE MANIFEST. THE GREEK WORD, <u>MANIFEST,</u> MEANS: OPEN TO SIGHT, VISIBLE, OR SHINING.

CHAPTER 1: THE JUDGMENT SEAT OF CHRIST

REVELATION 13:15 DO OUR WORKS GLORIFY CHRIST OR WILL THEY BE BURNED UP? WE WILL BE JUDGED ACCORDING TO <u>HOW WE BUILD UPON</u> THE FOUNDATION OF JESUS AND HIS WORDS. WILL WE RECEIVE REWARD OR WILL WE SUFFER LOSS? WE CANNOT REDEEM TIME. JUDGMENT IS COMING SOON. ONE REASON THAT I BELIEVE THIS IS THAT PORTIONS OF SCRIPTURE WHICH WE COULD NOT PREVIOUSLY UNDERSTAND ARE NOW BEING REVEALED TO US. FOR EXAMPLE, IN BOOK OF REVELATION GOD SPEAKS THROUGH JOHN IN REVELATION 13:15 SAYING:

> *Revelation 13:15* And he had power to give life unto the image of the beast, that the image of the beast should both speak, and cause that as many as would not worship the image of the beast should be killed.

REVELATION 9:3-11, REVELATION 19:20, REVELATION 20:10. UNTIL RECENTLY, NO ONE UNDERSTOOD THE "IMAGE" THAT COULD SPEAK AND KILL BECAUSE ONLY GOD CAN CREATE LIFE. NOW WE CAN WONDER IF IT COULD BE AN ARTIFICIALLY INTELLIGENT (AI) ROBOT (THAT CAN BE MADE TO LOOK LIKE A MAN OR "BEAST"). COULD THEY ALSO BE MADE TO SHOW EMOTION OR EVEN PAIN? SIMILARLY, THE STRANGE CREATURES IN REVELATION 9 THAT LOOK LIKE "LOCUSTS," MOST OF US THOUGHT WERE SYMBOLIC OF DEMONS OR WERE

ARE YOU READY?

ALLEGORICAL CREATURES. I SUGGEST THAT YOU GOOGLE "LOCUSTS, GRASSHOPPER, AND/OR SCORPION DRONES."

***Revelation 9:3-11** And there came out of the smoke locusts upon the earth: and unto them was given power, as the scorpions of the earth have power. **4** And it was commanded them that they should not hurt the grass of the earth, neither any green thing, neither any tree; but only those men which have not the seal of God in their foreheads. **5** And to them it was given that they should not kill them, but that they should be tormented five months: and their torment was as the torment of a scorpion, when he striketh a man. **6** And in those days shall men seek death, and shall not find it; and shall desire to die, and death shall flee from them. **7** And the shapes of the locusts were like unto horses prepared unto battle; and on their heads were as it were crowns like gold, and their faces were as the faces of men. **8** And they had hair as the hair of women, and their teeth were as the teeth of lions. **9** And they had breastplates, as it were breastplates of iron; and the sound of their wings was as the sound of chariots of many horses running to battle. **10** And they had tails like unto*

CHAPTER 1: THE JUDGMENT SEAT OF CHRIST

scorpions, and there were stings in their tails: and their power was to hurt men five months. **11** *And they had a king over them, which is the angel of the bottomless pit, whose name in the Hebrew tongue is Abaddon, but in the Greek tongue hath his name Apollyon.*

Revelation 19:20 *And the beast was taken, and with him the false prophet that wrought miracles before him, with which he deceived them that had received the mark of the beast, and them that worshipped his image. These both were cast alive into a lake of fire burning with brimstone.*

Revelation 20:10 *And the devil that deceived them was cast into the lake of fire and brimstone, where the beast and the false prophet are, and shall be tormented day and night for ever and ever.*

THESE LOCUST DRONES ARE UBIQUITOUS.

THIS ADDED TO THE OTHER NUMEROUS CURRENT EVENTS SEEMS TO INDICATE THAT THE CLOSE (END) OF THIS AGE IS VERY NEAR WHICH WILL CONCLUDE WITH THE RAPTURE OF THE CHURCH AND THEN COMES THE JUDGMENT!

COLOSSIANS 3:23-25. I BELIEVE JUDGMENT WILL REVEAL OUR MOTIVES FOR THE THINGS WE HAVE DONE (GOOD AND BAD) <u>AND ALL THOSE THINGS WHICH WE SHOULD HAVE DONE</u>. DID I LIVE FOR GOD AS A CHRISTIAN OR DID I LIVE FOR PLEASURE AND SELF-GRATIFICATION IN REBELLION AGAINST A HOLY GOD AND HIS WORDS?

Colossians 3:23-25 And whatsoever ye do, do it heartily, as to the Lord, and not unto men; 24 Knowing that of the Lord ye shall receive the reward of the inheritance: for ye serve the Lord Christ. 25 But he that doeth wrong shall receive for the wrong which he hath done: and there is no respect of persons.

FOR EVERY PROBLEM OR QUESTION THAT WE HAVE, THE BIBLE HAS THE ANSWER.

1 JOHN 3:4. SIN IS TRANSGRESSION OF THE LAW, GOD'S HOLY WORD.

1 John 3:4 Whosoever committeth sin transgresseth also the law: for sin is the transgression of the law.

THERE ARE TWO KINDS OF SIN; THOSE OF COMMISSION AND THOSE OF OMISSION. COMMISSION IS THE ONE WE NORMALLY JUDGE OURSELVES BY. IT IS DOING

CHAPTER 1: THE JUDGMENT SEAT OF CHRIST

ANYTHING FORBIDDEN BY THE LAW. DON'T LIE, STEAL, KILL, ETC.

OMISSION IS NOT DOING WHAT THE LAW REQUIRES SUCH AS LOVE YOUR NEIGHBOR, PRAY, STUDY THE WORD, KEEP ALL COMMANDMENTS, WITNESS, ETC. WE ARE COMMANDED TO OBEY BOTH. THE BIBLE SAYS THE WRATH OF GOD COMETH ON THE CHILDREN OF DISOBEDIENCE. GOD HATES SIN!! HE WILL JUDGE.

EPHESIANS 1:7; 2 CORINTHIANS 5:17-21. "REDEMPTION IS DELIVERANCE FROM BONDAGE BY MEANS OF A PRICE PAID." WE ARE BOUGHT OUT OF THE MARKET PLACE OF THE WORLD OF SIN BY THE PRICE PAID BY CHRIST'S PRECIOUS BLOOD. WE'VE BEEN BOUGHT AND PAID FOR BY THE BLOOD OF JESUS CHRIST AND RECONCILED TO GOD. WE ARE MADE AMBASSADORS FOR CHRIST AND SHOULD SERVE HIM. OUR SINS ARE FORGIVEN, COMPLETELY BLOTTED OUT, AND REMEMBERED NO MORE. THE RICHES OF GOD'S GRACE ARE INFINITE.

> *Ephesians 1:7* In whom we have redemption through his blood, the forgiveness of sins, according to the riches of his grace;
>
> *2 Corinthians 5:17* Therefore if any man be in Christ, he is a new creature: old things are passed away; behold, all things are become new. *18* And all things are of God, who hath

> *<u>reconciled</u> us to himself by Jesus Christ, and hath given to us the ministry of <u>reconciliation</u>;* **19** *To wit, that God was in Christ, <u>reconciling</u> the world unto himself, not imputing their trespasses unto them; and hath committed unto us the word of <u>reconciliation</u>.* **20** *Now then we are <u>ambassadors</u> for Christ, as though God did beseech you by us: we pray you in Christ's stead, be ye<u> reconciled</u> to God.* **21** *For he hath made him to be sin for us, who knew no sin; that we might be made the righteousness of God in him.*

AS BELIEVERS, WE BELONG TO GOD. EVEN THOUGH WE'RE HIS CHILDREN, HE IS OUR MASTER AND WE ARE HIS SERVANTS.

ROMANS 6:13, 16, 18. A SERVANT IN THIS SENSE IS ONE WHO PERFORMS SOME SERVICE, TASK, OR MISSION FOR THE LORD. MANY SAINTS IN THE OLD AND NEW TESTAMENTS ARE CALLED SERVANTS. CHRISTIANS ARE SERVANTS OF GOD WITHOUT THE IDEA OF BONDAGE. GOD SAYS YIELD YOUR BODIES INSTRUMENTS (OR SERVANTS) OF RIGHTEOUSNESS UNTO GOD.

> ***Romans 6:13*** *Neither yield ye your members as instruments of unrighteousness unto sin: but yield yourselves unto God, as those that are alive from the dead, and your*

CHAPTER 1: THE JUDGMENT SEAT OF CHRIST

members as instruments of righteousness unto God.

Romans 6:16 *Know ye not, that to whom ye yield yourselves servants to obey, his servants ye are to whom ye obey; whether of sin unto death, or of obedience unto righteousness?*

Romans 6:18 *Being then made free from sin, ye became the servants of righteousness.*

THE QUESTION IS "ARE WE GOOD AND FAITHFUL SERVANTS, OR ARE WE UNPROFITABLE SERVANTS?" WHAT DO YOU THINK GOD EXPECTS OF HIS SERVANTS?

ROMANS 12:1-2. PLEASE KEEP LOOKING AT YOUR BIBLE OR THE VERSES QUOTED AS WE STUDY THESE PASSAGES. BESEECH IN THE HEBREW MEANS TO BEG, IMPLORE, ENTREAT, ASK EARNESTLY. PAUL COULD NOT HAVE USED STRONGER LANGUAGE. IT MUST BE OF UTMOST IMPORTANCE; A WARNING TO GET STARTED WITHOUT DELAY. PAUL SAID "BY THE MERCIES OF GOD," THAT IS THOSE FREE AND UNMERITED GIFTS FROM GOD, LIKE THE REDEEMING OF OUR SOULS.

Romans 12:1-2 *I beseech you therefore, brethren, by the mercies of God, that ye present your bodies a living sacrifice, holy, acceptable unto*

*God, which is your reasonable service. **2** And be not conformed to this world: but be ye transformed by the renewing of your mind, that ye may prove what is that good, and acceptable, and perfect, will of God.*

HE SAID, "*THAT YE* (ALL OF US) *PRESENT* (OR YIELD) *YOUR BODIES* (YOUR LIFE) *A LIVING SACRIFICE.*" NOT A DEAD SACRIFICE. NOT A "LUKEWARM" SACRIFICE. A LIVING SACRIFICE FROM THE TIME WE ARE SAVED UNTIL OUR DEATH OR THE RAPTURE OF GOD'S CHURCH. WE OWE GOD <u>OUR ALL</u>! NOTHING HELD BACK.

PAUL SAID: "*HOLY, ACCEPTABLE UNTO GOD.*" ANIMAL SACRIFICES IN THE OLD TESTAMENT ACCOMPLISHED BY THE LAW WERE CONSIDERED HOLY. OUR SACRIFICE, IF ACCOMPLISHED IN ACCORDANCE WITH GOD'S WORD, IS ALSO CONSIDERED HOLY. SACRIFICES MADE OUTSIDE THE LAW WERE <u>NOT</u> ACCEPTABLE. THE QUESTION IS, WILL OUR SACRIFICES BE ACCEPTABLE OR UNACCEPTABLE?

PAUL SAID, "*WHICH IS OUR REASONABLE SERVICE.*" HE WAS IMPLYING INTELLIGENT AND SOUND SERVICE WITHIN THE SCOPE OF OUR CAPABILITY.

WE ARE TO PRESENT OUR ENTIRE LIFE TO THE LORD. WOW!!! THAT'S CONVICTING.

SEE VERSE 2 ABOVE IN ROMANS 12: "*AND BE NOT CONFORMED TO THIS*

CHAPTER 1: THE JUDGMENT SEAT OF CHRIST

WORLD." **A WORLD SYSTEM DOMINATED BY THE GOD OF THIS WORLD, SATAN HIMSELF. (EPHESIANS 2:2)**

***Ephesians 2:2** Wherein in time past ye walked according to the course of this world, according to the prince of the power of the air, the spirit that now worketh in the children of disobedience:*

PAUL SAID IN ROMANS 12:2 ABOVE: *"BUT BE YE TRANSFORMED."* HE IS REFERRING TO A PROCESS WHICH TAKES PLACE AS WE MATURE IN OUR SERVICE TO GOD. *"BE YE TRANSFORMED BY THE RENEWING OF YOUR MIND."* THAT IS A SPIRITUAL TRANSFORMATION THAT MAKES OUR LIFE NEW. IT IS ONE THAT CHANGES OUR ACTIONS, ATTITUDE, AND MOTIVES TOWARD GOD <u>AND</u> OUR SERVICE TO HIM.

PAUL CONCLUDES BY SAYING: *"THAT YE MAY <u>PROVE</u> WHAT IS THAT GOOD, AND ACCEPTABLE, AND PERFECT WILL OF GOD."* PROVE MEANS TO <u>PUT TO THE TEST</u> BY ACTIONS TO ACHIEVE <u>GOD'S</u> PURPOSE.

LUKE 9:23. JESUS TEACHES CHRISTIANS TO TAKE UP THEIR CROSS DAILY AND FOLLOW HIM. LIVE A LIFE OF SELF-DENIAL. DIE TO SELF AND SUFFER HARDSHIP AND PERSECUTION FOR THE CAUSE OF CHRIST. WE ARE TO LIVE FOR JESUS AND NOT FOR OURSELVES.

> *Luke 9:23 And he said to them all, If any man will come after me, let him deny himself, and take up his cross daily, and follow me.*

DAILY MEANS DAILY, NOT EVERY NOW AND THEN.

LUKE 14:27. I WANT TO BE A DISCIPLE OF JESUS. I WANT TO FOLLOW JESUS, BUT I FALL VERY SHORT OF HIS STANDARD. "*WHOSOEVER*" MEANS WHOEVER; THAT'S YOU AND ME. HE SAID BEAR OUR CROSS AND COME AFTER HIM OR WE <u>CANNOT</u> BE HIS DISCIPLE. "*BEAR*" IN THE GREEK MEANS TO TAKE UP AND HOLD. IT IS PUTTING THE WEIGHT LIKE JESUS BEARS ON OUR OWN SHOULDER.

> *Luke 14:27 And whosoever doth not bear his cross, and come after me, cannot be my disciple.*

A DISCIPLE IS ONE WHO <u>ACCEPTS</u> THE INSTRUCTIONS GIVEN TO HIM AND MAKES IT <u>HIS RULE OF CONDUCT</u>.

WHEN JESUS GAVE THESE EXPLICIT INSTRUCTIONS, A DISCIPLE FOLLOWING JESUS WAS LIKELY TO LOSE EVERYTHING, INCLUDING HIS LIFE AND THE LIVES OF HIS FAMILY. EVEN TODAY MANY CHRISTIANS ARE STILL BEING KILLED FOR THEIR FAITH.

"MARTYRS MIRROR," A BOOK BY THIELMAN J. VAN BRAGHT, IS THE STORY OF

CHAPTER 1: THE JUDGMENT SEAT OF CHRIST

SEVENTEEN CENTURIES OF CHRISTIAN MARTYRDOM, FROM THE TIME OF CHRIST TO 1660 A.D. IT RECORDS THOUSANDS OF CHRISTIANS WHO DIED FOLLOWING UNIMAGINABLE TORTURE FOR THE CAUSE OF CHRIST AND REFUSING TO DENY HIM.

WE HAVE IT MADE LIVING IN AMERICA. WHAT COULD IT POSSIBLY COST US TO FOLLOW JESUS? BEING MADE FUN OF OR RIDICULED? ONE DAY, I BELIEVE SOON, IT WILL COST MUCH MORE. IT MAKES ME WONDER HOW I'LL BE JUDGED ON BEING A DISCIPLE OF JESUS. TODAY WE HAVE TELEPHONES, COMPUTERS, VEHICLES, THE PRINTING PRESS, AND MUCH MORE FREE TIME, YET MOST OF US DON'T COME CLOSE TO THE SACRIFICES THAT PEOPLE IN OTHER COUNTRIES FACE DAILY.

LUKE 9:26. WE SHOULD NEVER BE ASHAMED OF CHRIST AND HIS GOSPEL. IT DOESN'T MEAN JUST EVERY NOW AND THEN ADMITTING WE ARE CHRISTIANS. IT MEANS LIVING FOR HIM!

HE GAVE IT ALL!!! WHAT DO WE GIVE? JESUS COULD COME FOR HIS CHURCH THIS VERY SECOND. WILL HE CATCH US NAPPING?

> *Luke 9:26* For whosoever shall be ashamed of me and of my words, of him shall the Son of man be ashamed, when he shall come in his own glory,

and in his Father's, and of the holy angels.

JOHN 5:22-23. GOD HAS COMMITTED ALL JUDGMENT UNTO JESUS WHO WILL JUDGE US BY HIS WORD. I CAN'T HELP BUT THINK THAT WE HAVE A TENDENCY <u>NOT</u> TO READ OR STUDY OUR BIBLE, NOT TO ATTEND CHURCH REGULARLY, AND NOT TO MEDITATE ON GOD'S WORD SO THAT BY NOT KNOWING WE WILL AVOID JUDGMENT. THIS CAN'T BE FURTHER FROM THE TRUTH. JESUS WILL JUDGE US BY HIS WORD, NOT OUR NEGLIGENCE. <u>IGNORANCE WILL NOT BE AN EXCUSE.</u>

***John 5:22** For the Father judgeth no man, but hath committed all judgment unto the Son: 23 That all men should honour the Son, even as they honour the Father. He that honoureth not the Son honoureth not the Father which hath sent him.*

THE JUDGMENT SEAT OF CHRIST SCARES ME BECAUSE OF MY LACK OF PREPARATION AND SERVICE TO MY HOLY GOD.

ROMANS 3:23. *"ALL HAVE SINNED AND COME <u>SHORT</u> OF THE GLORY OF GOD."* THAT'S YOU AND ME. WE'VE ALL MISSED THE MARK. AFTER WE'RE SAVED, OUR HIGH-WATER MARK SHOULD BE TO SERVE GOD TO THE VERY BEST OF OUR ABILITY.

CHAPTER 1: THE JUDGMENT SEAT OF CHRIST

***Romans 3:23** For all have sinned, and come short of the glory of God;*

JOHN 3:3. JESUS TOLD NICODEMUS, A RABBI, THAT EVERYONE MUST BE BORN AGAIN TO SEE THE KINGDOM OF GOD. WE MUST BE BORN INTO GOD'S FAMILY AS A NEW BABE IN CHRIST, IMMATURE IN THE KNOWLEDGE OF THE BIBLE.

***John 3:3** Jesus answered and said unto him, Verily, verily, I say unto thee, Except a man be born again, he cannot see the kingdom of God.*

1 PETER 2:2. WE SHOULD DESIRE THE PURE WORD OF GOD JUST LIKE A BABY DESIRES MILK.

***1 Peter 2:2** As newborn babes, desire the sincere milk of the word, that ye may grow thereby:*

THINK ABOUT A BABY AND HOW THEY CRY, PLEAD, AND BEG FOR MILK. THEY'RE ONLY CONTENT WHEN THEY HAVE THEIR FILL. IS IT <u>NOT</u> A COMMAND OF GOD TO DESIRE TO BE FILLED WITH HIS WORD(S)?

HEBREWS 5:12-14. HOW LONG HAVE YOU AND I FED ON GOOD PREACHING? MOST OF US WOULD HAVE TO SAY MANY YEARS. ARE WE STILL JUST HEARERS OF THE WORD AND <u>NOT</u> DOERS?

> *Hebrews 5:12-14 For when for the time ye ought to be teachers, ye have need that one teach you again which be the first principles of the oracles of God; and are become such as have need of milk, and not of strong meat. 13 For every one that useth milk is unskilful in the word of righteousness: for he is a babe. 14 But strong meat belongeth to them that are of full age, even those who by reason of use have their senses exercised to discern both good and evil.*

JAMES 1:22. AT A TIME WHEN WE SHOULD BE TEACHING OTHERS, ARE WE? MUST WE ALWAYS HAVE NEED OF MILK AND MEET GOD'S JUDGMENT AS A BABE IN CHRIST? DOESN'T IMMATURE ALSO APPLY TO OUR SERVICE FOR GOD?

> *James 1:22 But be ye doers of the word, and not hearers only, deceiving your own selves.*

ROMANS 8:14. THE WORD "LED" IN THE BIBLE HAS MULTIPLE MEANINGS, BUT FOR MY PURPOSE BELOW I USE "BRING INTO SUBJECTION, LAYING HOLD UPON THAT WHICH IS PRESENTED, OR LED BY THE HAND." IF WE ARE LED BY THE SPIRIT OF GOD THEN WE ARE THE SONS OF GOD. WHAT IF WE ARE NOT LED BY THE SPIRIT OF GOD?

CHAPTER 1: THE JUDGMENT SEAT OF CHRIST

A FEW YEARS AGO WHILE DOOR KNOCKING WITH A PASTOR FRIEND WE DROVE UP A DRIVEWAY WHICH HAD A HOUSE ON BOTH SIDES. BOTH HOUSES LOOKED PEACEFUL, BUT IN THE YARD OF THE HOUSE ON THE RIGHT WERE TWO LARGE DOGS. THEY WERE BARKING AND GROWLING AND APPEARED TO HAVE PERFECT TEETH. THEY LET IT BE KNOWN THAT THEIR DESIRE WAS TO EAT US. THEY APPEARED TO BE CONSTRAINED IN THEIR YARD BY A HIDDEN ELECTRONIC DEVICE. I SAID, "PASTOR, YOU GET THE HOUSE ON THE RIGHT AND I'LL GET THE ONE ON THE LEFT". HIS CLASSIC ANSWER WAS "I DON'T FEEL '<u>LED</u>' TO GET THAT HOUSE". I HAD TO CONFESS I DIDN'T EITHER. I HOPE GOD WILL FORGIVE OUR NEGLIGENCE.

I ONCE HEARD A LONG TIME CHURCH MEMBER WHEN INVITED TO GO SOUL WINNING REPLY THAT HE DIDN'T FEEL "<u>LED</u>" TO GO. I WONDERED IF HE WAS WAITING ON AN ANGEL WITH A LEASH OR SOME OTHER REINFORCEMENT RATHER THAN GOD'S VERY CLEAR WRITTEN WORD.

UPON FURTHER REFLECTION I REALIZED I HAD THE GREATER PROBLEM. I WILL GIVE ACCOUNT FOR MY <u>OWN</u> SHORTCOMINGS AND MY <u>OWN</u> LACK OF SERVICE TO GOD.

NO BORN AGAIN CHRISTIAN NEEDS TO BE <u>LED</u> EXCEPT BY THE HOLY SPIRIT, AND

THE CLEARLY REVEALED WORD OF GOD. GOD'S WORD IS ALL SUFFICIENT.

Romans 8:14 For as many as are led by the Spirit of God, they are the sons of God.

LUKE 17:7-10. THIS PARABLE REFLECTS ON OUR ATTITUDE. IF WE <u>ONLY</u> DO WHAT GOD COMMANDS US TO DO, THEN <u>ARE WE NOT</u> UNPROFITABLE SERVANTS?

Luke 17:7-10 But which of you, having a servant plowing or feeding cattle, will say unto him by and by, when he is come from the field, Go and sit down to meat? 8 And will not rather say unto him, Make ready wherewith I may sup, and gird thyself, and serve me, till I have eaten and drunken; and afterward thou shalt eat and drink? 9 Doth he thank that servant because he did the things that were commanded him? I trow not. 10 So likewise ye, when ye shall have done all those things which are commanded you, say, We are unprofitable servants: we have done that which was our duty to do.

IN THIS SENSE WE HAVE NOT PROFITED OR BENEFITTED GOD. WE SHOULD GO THE EXTRA MILE. (MATTHEW 5:41)

CHAPTER 1: THE JUDGMENT SEAT OF CHRIST

> ***Matthew 5:41*** *And whosoever shall compel thee to go a mile, go with him twain.*

THE WORD OF GOD REVEALS NUMEROUS TASKS WHICH WE SHOULD PERFORM NOT TO BE ONE OF THE "<u>**UNPROFITABLE**</u>" SERVANTS. THAT IS DOING <u>ONLY</u> THOSE THINGS WHICH ARE IN OUR ABILITY TO DO. WE'LL LOOK AT <u>ONLY</u> A FEW.

REVELATION 4:10-11. WORSHIP IS REVERENT DEVOTION AND ALLEGIANCE PLEDGED TO GOD. IT'S TO ADORE, AND TO DO OBEISANCE. GOD CREATED <u>ALL</u> THINGS (THAT INCLUDES US) FOR HIS PLEASURE, NOT OURS. WHEN WE SEE JESUS AT THE JUDGMENT SEAT I BELIEVE WE WILL FALL PROSTRATE WITH SHAME AND OUR FACE IN THE DIRT, (SO TO SPEAK), KNOWING THAT WE HAVE MISSED MANY OPPORTUNITIES TO SERVE OUR GOD.

> ***Revelation 4:10-11*** *The four and twenty elders fall down before him that sat on the throne, and worship him that liveth for ever and ever, and cast their crowns before the throne, saying,* **11** *Thou art worthy, O Lord, to receive glory and honour and power: for thou hast created all things, and for thy pleasure they are and were created.*

ARE YOU READY?

JOHN 14:15. IS OUR HEART FILLED WITH LOVE FOR CHRIST SO THAT WE WILL KEEP <u>ALL</u> OF HIS COMMANDMENTS? THERE ARE MANY. ONE COULD ASK WHY DO WE CONTINUE TO DO OUR OWN THING RATHER THAN OBEY THE WILL OF GOD?

John 14:15 If ye love me, keep my commandments.

DEUTERONOMY 5:1, 7:12, 26:16. MUCH OF THE BIBLE IS WRITTEN TO THE JEWS BUT ALL SCRIPTURE HAS APPLICATION TO EVERYONE, BOTH JEW AND GENTILE. GOD SAYS TO <u>LEARN</u> HIS STATUTES AND JUDGMENTS AND <u>KEEP</u> AND <u>DO</u> THEM WITH ALL THY HEART AND ALL THY SOUL. IF WE WILL, GOD WILL KEEP ALL HIS NUMEROUS PROMISES TO US.

Deuteronomy 5:1 And Moses called all Israel, and said unto them, Hear, O Israel, the statutes and judgments which I speak in your ears this day, that ye may learn them, and keep, and do them.

Deuteronomy 7:12 Wherefore it shall come to pass, if ye hearken to these judgments, and keep, and do them, that the LORD thy God shall keep unto thee the covenant and the mercy which he sware unto thy fathers:

CHAPTER 1: THE JUDGMENT SEAT OF CHRIST

Deuteronomy 26:16 This day the LORD thy God hath commanded thee to do these statutes and judgments: thou shalt therefore keep and do them with all thine heart, and with all thy soul.

1 THESSALONIANS 5:17. PRAY WITHOUT CEASING OR PRAY WITHOUT INTERMISSIONS. THE MEANING IS <u>NOT</u> THAT WE SHOULD NOT DO ANYTHING BUT PRAY, BUT THAT NOTHING SHOULD HINDER OUR PRAYER AT ITS PROPER TIME. WE SHOULD BE IN A STATE OF PRAYER SEEKING GOD'S WILL IN ALL THAT WE DO. DO WE REALLY PRAY LIKE WE ARE COMMANDED TO DO?

1 Thessalonians 5:17 Pray without ceasing.

II TIMOTHY 2:15. STUDY IN THE GREEK MEANS TO BE DILIGENT. DON'T JUST READ IT. ACQUIRE KNOWLEDGE, BE EARNEST, INVESTIGATE, MEDITATE, AND <u>USE</u> IT.

2 Timothy 2:15 Study to shew thyself approved unto God, a workman that needeth not to be ashamed, rightly dividing the word of truth.

THYSELF MEANS YOU AND ME. WORKMAN MEANS <u>WORK</u> AT IT. DON'T BE

ASHAMED OF IT. THE MORE WE STUDY, THE MORE WE UNDERSTAND.

I WAS SAVED IN 1969. I'VE BEEN FED BY MANY GREAT PREACHERS, AND THAT CONTINUES. I'VE EVEN READ THE BIBLE AND STUDIED A LITTLE. BUT I AM AFRAID THAT WHEN I AM JUDGED I WILL HAVE TO ANSWER AS TO WHY I KEPT THIS KNOWLEDGE TO MYSELF, TOO ASHAMED OR LAZY TO SHARE IT WITH OTHERS. AFTER ALL I HAVE A FAMILY. I HAD TO WORK. I WAS TOO TIRED. I'M JUST TOO BUSY. DOES THIS SOUND FAMILIAR?

MATTHEW 28:18-20. WHY WOULD JESUS LEAVE US HERE ON EARTH AFTER WE'RE SAVED? IT IS TO KEEP HIS WORD. *"ALL POWER"* OF JESUS IS **ALL** THE AUTHORITY THAT WE NEED TO ACCOMPLISH HIS COMMANDMENTS. *"GO YE"* IN THE GREEK MEANS THAT WE **WILL** AUTOMATICALLY BE GOING. IN OTHER WORDS "AS YOU ARE GOING."

> *Matthew 28:18-20 And Jesus came and spake unto them, saying, All power is given unto me in heaven and in earth. **19** Go ye therefore, and teach all nations, baptizing them in the name of the Father, and of the Son, and of the Holy Ghost: **20** Teaching them to observe all things whatsoever I have commanded you:*

CHAPTER 1: THE JUDGMENT SEAT OF CHRIST

and, lo, I am with you alway, even unto the end of the world. Amen.

LUKE 14:23. TO DO WHAT? TO GET PEOPLE SAVED, BAPTIZED, AND TEACH THEM TO OBSERVE ALL THINGS. COMPEL THEM TO COME IN.

Luke 14:23 And the lord said unto the servant, Go out into the highways and hedges, and compel them to come in, that my house may be filled.

THIS IS <u>NOT</u> AN OPTION, IT IS A COMMAND.

JOHN 15:20. WE ARE SERVANTS OF OUR LORD AND SAVIOUR JESUS CHRIST. GOD'S WORD SAYS <u>IF WE SERVE HIM WE WILL SUFFER PERSECUTION</u>. TO SUFFER PERSECUTION WE MUST KEEP JESUS' SAYINGS. DO WE? <u>NOT</u> DOING SO COULD BE SOME OF THE "BAD" THAT WE MUST ANSWER FOR AT THE JUDGMENT SEAT OF CHRIST.

John 15:20 Remember the word that I said unto you, The servant is not greater than his lord. If they have persecuted me, they will also persecute you; if they have kept my saying, they will keep yours also.

WE COULD GO ON FOREVER STUDYING OUR <u>LACK</u> OF SERVICE TO OUR HOLY GOD.

WHEN I MEET JESUS AT THE JUDGMENT SEAT OF CHRIST, WILL THE LITTLE THAT I THINK I'VE ACCOMPLISHED REALLY BRING GLORY, HONOR, AND PRAISE TO MY HOLY GOD? I BELIEVE MY "BAD" WILL INCLUDE MY LACK OF SERVICE, MY MOTIVES, AND MY FAILURE TO KEEP <u>ALL</u> OF GOD'S COMMANDMENTS TO THE VERY BEST OF MY ABILITY. THIS IS A FRIGHTENING THOUGHT FOR ME. WHAT ABOUT YOU?

OUR SINS <u>ARE</u> GONE BUT WE <u>WILL</u> BE JUDGED FOR BOTH THE "GOOD AND THE BAD."

CHAPTER 2
THE GREAT WHITE THRONE JUDGMENT

THE GREAT WHITE THRONE JUDGMENT IS A PLACE WHERE PEOPLE WHO HAVE NOT PUT THEIR TRUST AND FAITH IN CHRIST JESUS WILL BE JUDGED. ALL ARE LOST AND WILL BE CAST INTO A LAKE OF FIRE. THEY WILL BE TORMENTED DAY AND NIGHT FOREVER AND EVER, ETERNALLY SEPARATED FROM GOD, TOO LATE FOR ANY MERCY. THEY HAVE ABSOLUTELY NO HOPE. "... AS IT IS APPOINTED UNTO MEN ONCE TO DIE, BUT AFTER THIS THE JUDGMENT" (HEBREWS 9:27).

TO SET THE STAGE FOR A STUDY OF "THE GREAT WHITE THRONE JUDGMENT" WE NEED TO ESTABLISH A FEW RELATED BIBLE TRUTHS.

2 PETER 2:1-4. THERE HAVE ALWAYS BEEN FALSE PROPHETS THAT BRING IN DAMNABLE HERESIES. SOME EVEN DENY GOD.

> *2 Peter 2:1-4 But there were false prophets also among the people, even as there shall be false teachers among you, who privily shall bring in damnable heresies, even denying the Lord that bought them, and bring upon themselves swift destruction. 2*

And many shall follow their pernicious ways; by reason of whom the way of truth shall be evil spoken of. ***3*** *And through covetousness shall they with feigned words make merchandise of you: whose judgment now of a long time lingereth not, and their damnation slumbereth not.* ***4*** *For if God spared not the angels that sinned, but cast them down to hell, and delivered them into chains of darkness, to be reserved unto judgment;*

2 PETER 3:9. SEVERAL YEARS AGO, THE HEADLINE IN AN ARTICLE IN THE ATLANTA JOURNAL SAID: "GOD IS DEAD." THE ARTICLE QUOTED A PROFESSOR AT EMORY UNIVERSITY. TODAY MANY PEOPLE ARE STILL DENYING THE TRUTHS IN THE BIBLE, AND MANY BELIEVE THAT GOD IS DEAD. GOD IS NOT DEAD! HE IS LONGSUFFERING, BUT HIS JUDGMENT WILL COME SWIFTLY AND SURELY.

2 Peter 3:9* The Lord is not slack concerning his promise, as some men count slackness; but is longsuffering to us-ward, not willing that any should perish, but that all should come to repentance.*

2 PETER 2:3, 2 CORINTHIANS 4:3-4. REMEMBER, JUDGMENT CAME IN NOAH'S DAY AND IN LOT'S DAY, AND MANY OTHER

CHAPTER 2: THE GREAT WHITE THRONE JUDGMENT

JUDGMENTS OF BOTH THE JEWS AND GENTILES ARE RECORDED. GOD'S JUDGMENT "LINGERETH," BUT IT "SLUMBERETH NOT."

*2 Peter 2:3 And through covetousness shall they with feigned words make merchandise of you: whose judgment now of a long time **lingereth** not, and their damnation **slumbereth** not.*

LOOK AT THESE VERSES:

2 Corinthians 4:3-4 But if our gospel be hid, it is hid to them that are lost: 4 In whom the god of this world hath blinded the minds of them which believe not, lest the light of the glorious gospel of Christ, who is the image of God, should shine unto them.

2 PETER 2:4. FURTHERMORE, GOD SPARED NOT THE ANGELS THAT SINNED, BUT CAST THEM IN CHAINS OF DARKNESS TO HELL WAITING ON THEIR FINAL g69 JUDGMENT.

2 Peter 2:4 For if God spared not the angels that sinned, but cast them down to hell, and delivered them into chains of darkness, to be reserved unto judgment;

1 TIMOTHY 4:1. GOD'S JUDGMENT IS SURE. DENYING JESUS WILL SURELY SEND

DENIERS TO THE GREAT WHITE THRONE JUDGMENT.

NOTICE IN 2 CORINTHIANS 4:3-4, ABOVE, THAT THE GOD OF THIS WORLD, SATAN, HAS BLINDED THE MINDS OF MEN FOR AGES. HE DOES <u>NOT</u> WANT PEOPLE TO KNOW THE TRUTH.

SATAN, WITH HIS DEMONS, HAS A VERY POWERFUL INFLUENCE ON THE AFFAIRS OF THIS WORLD. HIS GOAL IS TO DEFEAT ALL THAT JESUS CHRIST REPRESENTS.

> ***1 Timothy 4:1*** *Now the Spirit speaketh expressly, that in the latter times some shall depart from the faith, giving heed to seducing spirits, and doctrines of devils;*

IN MATTHEW 3:16-17, HE EVEN ATTEMPTS TO MIMIC GOD. OUR GODHEAD EXISTS IN <u>THREE PERSONS</u>, GOD THE FATHER, GOD THE SON, AND GOD THE HOLY SPIRIT, WHO ARE DISTINCT PERSONS, BUT OF THE SAME ESSENCE; THAT IS, THEY ARE EACH GOD, AND THEY ARE IN COMPLETE AGREEMENT AND THEREFORE CALLED ONE.

> ***Matthew 3:16-17*** *And **<u>Jesus</u>**, when he was baptized, went up straightway out of the water: and, lo, the heavens were opened unto him, and he saw the **<u>Spirit of God</u>** descending like a dove, and lighting upon him:* ***17*** *And*

*lo a **voice from heaven**, saying, This is **my beloved Son**, in whom I am well pleased.*

***Deuteronomy 6:4-5** Hear, O Israel: The LORD our God is **one** LORD: **5** And thou shalt love the LORD thy God with all thine heart, and with all thy soul, and with all thy might.*

DEUTERONOMY 6:4-5. THIS PASSAGE CLEARLY STATES THAT THERE IS ONLY ONE GOD, BUT HE EXISTS AS THREE PERSONS. THE JEWISH PEOPLE CALL THIS PASSAGE (6:4-9) THE SHEMA. TO THEM IT DEFINES THEIR GOD AS ONE GOD BUT IT HAS A DEEPER MEANING. THE WORD LORD (JEHOVAH) MEANS THE ETERNAL SELF-EXISTANT ONE. THE WORD GOD (ELOHIM) IS A PLURAL WORD FOR THE SUPREME GOD. HENCE, GOD IS ONE BUT EXISTS IN MORE THAN ONE DISTINCT PERSON.

NOTE THAT SATAN, GOD'S ENEMY, IS WORKING TOWARD HIS FALSE TRINITY: (1) THE DRAGON OR ANTIGOD; (2) THE BEAST OR ANTICHRIST; AND (3) THE FALSE PROPHET OR ANTISPIRIT (See Revelation 13:1-18).

COLOSSIANS 1:18. BE AWARE THAT IN COLOSSIANS 1:18 CHRIST HAS HIS CHURCH, THE ASSEMBLY OR BODY OF BELIEVERS.

***Colossians 1:18** And he is the head of the body, the church: who is the* *beginning, the firstborn from the dead; that in all things he might have the preeminence.*

REVELATION 2:9, REVELATION 3:9. SATAN HAS HIS CHURCH ALSO, CALLED THE SYNAGOGUE OF SATAN (AN ASSEMBLY OF UNBELIEVERS).

***Revelation 2:9** I know thy works, and tribulation, and poverty, (but thou art rich) and I know the blasphemy of them which say they are Jews, and are not, but are **the synagogue of Satan**.*

***Revelation 3:9** Behold, I will make them of **the synagogue of Satan**, which say they are Jews, and are not, but do lie; behold, I will make them to come and worship before thy feet, and to know that I have loved thee.*

1 CORINTHIANS 10:21. GOD HAS HIS CUP, THE COMMUNION CUP. SATAN HAS HIS CUP, THE CUP OF DEVILS.

***1 Corinthians 10:21** Ye cannot drink the cup of the Lord, and **the cup of devils**: ye cannot be partakers of the Lord's table, and of the table of devils.*

DANIEL 12:11. CHRIST'S MINISTRY LASTED THREE AND ONE-HALF YEARS. SATAN'S COUNTERFEIT MINISTRY WILL

CHAPTER 2: THE GREAT WHITE THRONE JUDGMENT

LAST THREE AND ONE-HALF YEARS DURING THE LAST HALF OF THE TRIBULATION. (THE PROOF OF THIS IS FOUND IN THE BOOK OF DANIEL CHAPTERS 9 AND 12.

> ***Daniel 12:11*** *And from the time that the daily sacrifice shall be taken away, and the abomination that maketh desolate set up, there shall be a thousand two hundred and ninety days.*

REVELATION 20:10. DO NOT BE FOOLED BY SATAN'S LIES. HE WILL BE DEFEATED AND CAST INTO THE LAKE OF FIRE.

> ***Revelation 20:10*** *And the devil that deceived them was cast into the lake of fire and brimstone, where the beast and the false prophet are, and shall be tormented day and night for ever and ever.*

MATTHEW 25:41. GOD PREPARED HELL FOR THE DEVIL AND HIS ANGELS.

> ***Matthew 25:41*** *Then shall he say also unto them on the left hand, Depart from me, ye cursed, into everlasting fire, **prepared** for the devil and his angels:*

JOHN 14:1-3. HE PREPARED HEAVEN FOR PEOPLE.

ARE YOU READY?

John 14:1 Let not your heart be troubled: ye believe in God, believe also in me. *2* In my Father's house are many mansions: if it were not so, I would have told you. I go to prepare a place for you. *3* And if I go and prepare a place for you, I will come again, and receive you unto myself; that where I am, there ye may be also.

BUT JESUS SAID YOU WILL NOT COME TO ME THAT YOU MIGHT HAVE LIFE. YOU CAN MISS THE GREAT WHITE THRONE JUDGMENT IF YOU WILL COME TO CHRIST.

1 Corinthians 10:21 Ye cannot drink the cup of the Lord, and the cup of devils: ye cannot be partakers of the Lord's table, and of the table of devils.

LUKE 16:13. YOU CANNOT SERVE TWO MASTERS. WE EITHER SERVE CHRIST OR SATAN. THERE IS NO FENCE STRADDLING.

Luke 16:13 No servant can serve two masters: for either he will hate the one, and love the other; or else he will hold to the one, and despise the other. Ye cannot serve God and mammon.

LUKE 16:19-31. THE RICH MAN DIED IN HIS SINS AND WAS TORMENTED. HE DESIRED JUST A WET FINGER TO TOUCH HIS

CHAPTER 2: THE GREAT WHITE THRONE JUDGMENT

TONGUE. HE REMEMBERED HIS LOST BROTHERS WITH COMPASSION. HE HAD <u>NO</u> HOPE...<u>NO</u> SECOND CHANCE...<u>NO</u> DO- OVER. HIS JUDGMENT WAS SEALED. EVEN TODAY 2,000 YEARS LATER, HE IS STILL IN TORMENT WAITING ON THAT DREADFUL DAY OF HIS FINAL JUDGMENT AT "THE GREAT WHITE THRONE JUDGMENT" WHERE HE WILL BOW TO JESUS AND RECEIVE HIS JUST PUNISHMENT FOR REJECTING ETERNAL LIFE THROUGH THE BLOOD OF JESUS CHRIST. ALL HOPE IS GONE FOR ALL ETERNITY. HE <u>MISSED</u> THE GREATEST GIFT EVER OFFERED.

> ***Luke 16:19*** *There was a certain rich man, which was clothed in purple and fine linen, and fared sumptuously every day:* ***20*** *And there was a certain beggar named Lazarus, which was laid at his gate, full of sores,* ***21*** *And desiring to be fed with the crumbs which fell from the rich man's table: moreover the dogs came and licked his sores.* ***22*** *And it came to pass, that the beggar died, and was carried by the angels into Abraham's bosom: the rich man also died, and was buried;* ***23*** *And in hell he lift up his eyes, being in torments, and seeth Abraham afar off, and Lazarus in his bosom.* ***24*** *And he cried and said, Father Abraham, have mercy on me, and send Lazarus, that he may dip the*

tip of his finger in water, and cool my tongue; for I am tormented in this flame. **25** *But Abraham said, Son, remember that thou in thy lifetime receivedst thy good things, and likewise Lazarus evil things: but now he is comforted, and thou art tormented.* **26** *And beside all this, between us and you there is a great gulf fixed: so that they which would pass from hence to you cannot; neither can they pass to us, that would come from thence.* **27** *Then he said, I pray thee therefore, father, that thou wouldest send him to my father's house:* **28** *For I have five brethren; that he may testify unto them, lest they also come into this place of torment.* **29** *Abraham saith unto him, They have Moses and the prophets; let them hear them.* **30** *And he said, Nay, father Abraham: but if one went unto them from the dead, they will repent.* **31** *And he said unto him, If they hear not Moses and the prophets, neither will they be persuaded, though one rose from the dead.*

REVELATION 19:11-21. THE APOSTLE JOHN SAID "I SAW." GOD BLESSED HIM BY LETTING HIM SEE OVER 2,000 YEARS INTO THE FUTURE.

LOOK AT WHAT HE SAW:

CHAPTER 2: THE GREAT WHITE THRONE JUDGMENT

HE SAW JESUS MAKING WAR ON EVIL PEOPLE.

HE SAW ARMIES OF SAINTS FOLLOWING JESUS.

HE SAW SATAN'S ARMIES DEFEATED AND BEING EATEN BY THE FOWLS OF THE AIR.

HE SAW THE BEAST AND FALSE PROPHET AND THOSE WHO HAD THE MARK OF THE BEAST AND THOSE WHO WORSHIPPED HIS IMAGE CAST ALIVE INTO THE LAKE OF FIRE.

HE WAS LOOKING AT HISTORY AS IT WILL HAPPEN AT THE END OF THE TRIBULATION. THIS IS JUST THE BEGINNING OF WHAT HE SAW.

> *Revelation 19:11-21* And I saw heaven opened, and behold a white horse; and he that sat upon him was called Faithful and True, and in righteousness he doth judge and make war. *12* His eyes were as a flame of fire, and on his head were many crowns; and he had a name written, that no man knew, but he himself. *13* And he was clothed with a vesture dipped in blood: and his name is called The Word of God. *14* And the armies which were in heaven followed him upon white horses, clothed in fine linen, white and clean. *15* And out of his mouth goeth a sharp sword, that

with it he should smite the nations: and he shall rule them with a rod of iron: and he treadeth the winepress of the fierceness and wrath of Almighty God. **16** And he hath on his vesture and on his thigh a name written, KING OF KINGS, AND LORD OF LORDS. **17** And I saw an angel standing in the sun; and he cried with a loud voice, saying to all the fowls that fly in the midst of heaven, Come and gather yourselves together unto the supper of the great God; **18** That ye may eat the flesh of kings, and the flesh of captains, and the flesh of mighty men, and the flesh of horses, and of them that sit on them, and the flesh of all men, both free and bond, both small and great. **19** And I saw the beast, and the kings of the earth, and their armies, gathered together to make war against him that sat on the horse, and against his army. **20** And the beast was taken, and with him the false prophet that wrought miracles before him, with which he deceived them that had received the mark of the beast, and them that worshipped his image. These both were cast alive into a lake of fire burning with brimstone. **21** And the remnant were slain with the sword of him that sat upon the horse, which sword

CHAPTER 2: THE GREAT WHITE THRONE JUDGMENT

proceeded out of his mouth: and all the fowls were filled with their flesh.

REVELATION 20:1-3. NEXT JOHN SAW AN ANGEL CHAIN THE BEAST (SATAN) AND CAST HIM INTO THE BOTTOMLESS PIT WHERE HE COULD NOT SOW HIS EVIL FOR 1,000 YEARS.

***Revelation 20:1-3** And I saw an angel come down from heaven, having the key of the bottomless pit and a great chain in his hand. **2** And he laid hold on the dragon, that old serpent, which is the Devil, and Satan, and bound him a thousand years, **3** And cast him into the bottomless pit, and shut him up, and set a seal upon him, that he should deceive the nations no more, till the thousand years should be fulfilled: and after that he must be loosed a little season.*

(SEE REVELATION 20:2 ABOVE.) JESUS WILL THEN ESTABLISH HIS "KINGDOM" AND RULE WITH HIS SAINTS FOR 1,000 YEARS AND AT THE END OF THE THOUSAND YEARS THE GREAT WHITE THRONE JUDGMENT WILL TAKE PLACE.

GALATIANS 5:19-21, LUKE 13:3, JOHN 3:16, JOHN 6:27, 47. YOU CAN AVOID THE GREAT WHITE THRONE JUDGMENT AND BE PART OF THE KINGDOM IF YOU WILL TURN

FROM THE WORLD, THE SINS OF THE FLESH, RESIST THE DEVIL, REPENT, AND PUT YOUR TRUST, FAITH, AND BELIEF IN JESUS CHRIST.

Galatians 5:19-21. Now the works of the flesh are manifest, which are these; Adultery, fornication, uncleanness, lasciviousness, **20** Idolatry, witchcraft, hatred, variance, emulations, wrath, strife, seditions, heresies, **21** Envyings, murders, drunkenness, revellings, and such like: of the which I tell you before, as I have also told you in time past, that they which do such things shall not inherit the kingdom of God.

Luke 13:3 I tell you, Nay: but, except ye repent, ye shall all likewise perish. (Luke 13:5)

John 3:16 For God so loved the world, that he gave his only begotten Son, that whosoever believeth in him should not perish, but have everlasting life.

John 6:27 Labour not for the meat which perisheth, but for that meat which endureth unto everlasting life, which the Son of man shall give unto you: for him hath God the Father sealed.

CHAPTER 2: THE GREAT WHITE THRONE JUDGMENT

John 6:47 *Verily, verily, I say unto you, <u>He that believeth on me hath everlasting life.</u>*

1 THESSALONIANS 4:13-17, MATTHEW 25:31, REVELATION 20:2. AFTER THE RAPTURE OF THE CHURCH AND THE END OF THE TRIBULATION THE MILLENNIAL REIGN OF CHRIST WILL OCCUR. YOU WOULD THINK THAT WITH SATAN CHAINED AND JESUS IN CONTROL, PEOPLE WOULD <u>NOT</u> SIN, BUT THEY WILL. MANY WILL REBEL AGAINST GOD. HE WILL PROVE WITHOUT ANY DOUBT THAT PEOPLE ARE NOT CAPABLE OF LIVING WITHOUT SIN AS LONG AS THEY POSSESS THEIR SIN NATURE. MAN HAS FAILED IN EVERY DISPENSATION. WE ARE <u>NOW</u> FAILING IN THIS DISPENSATION OF "GRACE" AND <u>WILL</u> FAIL IN THE DISPENSATION OF THE "KINGDOM."

***1 Thessalonians 4:13-17** But I would not have you to be ignorant, brethren, concerning them which are asleep, that ye sorrow not, even as others which have no hope. **14** For if we believe that Jesus died and rose again, even so them also which sleep in Jesus will God bring with him. **15** For this we say unto you by the word of the Lord, that we which are alive and remain unto the coming of the Lord shall not prevent them which are asleep. **16** For the Lord himself shall descend from heaven with a shout,* with the voice of the archangel, and with the trump of God: and the dead in Christ shall rise first: **17** Then we which are alive and remain shall be caught up together with them in the clouds, to meet the Lord in the air: and so shall we ever be with the Lord.

Matthew 25:31 When the Son of man shall come in his glory, and all the holy angels with him, then shall he sit upon the throne of his glory:

Revelation 20:2 And he laid hold on the dragon, that old serpent, which is the Devil, and Satan, and bound him a thousand years, *3* And cast him into the bottomless pit, and shut him up, and set a seal upon him, that he should deceive the nations no more, till the thousand years should be fulfilled: and after that he must be loosed a little season.

1 PETER 5:8, REVELATION 20:8. CAN YOU IMAGINE SATAN'S WRATH BUILDING UP WHILE BEING CHAINED AND TORMENTED FOR 1,000 YEARS? HE IS LIKE A "ROARING LION" NOW. WHAT WILL HE BE LIKE THEN? EVEN SO THOSE THAT WILL FOLLOW HIM WILL BE IN NUMBER LIKE SAND ON THE SEASHORE.

1 Peter 5:8. Be sober, be vigilant; because your adversary the devil, as a

CHAPTER 2: THE GREAT WHITE THRONE JUDGMENT

roaring lion, walketh about, seeking whom he may devour:

Revelation 20:8 *And shall go out to deceive the nations which are in the four quarters of the earth, Gog and Magog, to gather them together to battle: the number of whom is as the sand of the sea.*

EPHESIANS 2:8-9. IT IS AMAZING THAT A HOLY GOD (BY HIS GRACE) WOULD CONSIDER REDEEMING OUR SOULS.

Ephesians 2:8-9 *For by grace are ye saved through faith; and that not of yourselves: it is the gift of God:* **9** *Not of works, lest any man should boast.*

1 PETER 2:24, JAMES 2:19. HE DEMONSTRATED HIS LOVE ON THE CROSS OF CALVARY. WHY WON'T WE BELIEVE AND TRUST JESUS AND MISS THE GREAT WHITE THRONE JUDGMENT? WHY? REMEMBER, EVEN THE DEVILS BELIEVE AND TREMBLE.

1 Peter 2:24 *Who his own self bare our sins in his own body on the tree, that we, being dead to sins, should live unto righteousness: by whose stripes ye were healed.*

James 2:19 *Thou believest that there is one God; thou doest well: the devils also believe, and tremble.*

MATTHEW 22:37. BELIEVING CAN NOT SIMPLY BE A HEAD KNOWLEDGE ABOUT JESUS CHRIST. YOU CAN KNOW ABOUT JESUS AND NOT BE SAVED. YOU MUST TRUST HIM AND COMMIT YOUR LIFE TO HIM, COMPLETELY TRUSTING HIM WITH ALL YOUR HEART.

Matthew 22:37 Jesus said unto him, Thou shalt love the Lord thy God with all thy heart, and with all thy soul, and with all thy mind.

REVELATION 20:7-10. AFTER THE THOUSAND YEARS ARE OVER, SATAN WILL BE CAST INTO THE LAKE OF FIRE WHERE THE BEAST AND FALSE PROPHET ARE— TORMENTED DAY AND NIGHT FOREVER AND EVER. THEIR DEMONIC INFLUENCE WILL BE GONE FOREVER.

*Revelation 20:7-10 And when the thousand years are expired, Satan shall be loosed out of his prison, **8** And shall go out to deceive the nations which are in the four quarters of the earth, Gog and Magog, to gather them together to battle: the number of whom is as the sand of the sea. **9** And they went up on the breadth of the earth, and compassed the camp of the saints about, and the beloved city: and fire came down from God out of heaven, and devoured them. **10** And the devil that deceived*

CHAPTER 2: THE GREAT WHITE THRONE JUDGMENT

them was cast into the lake of fire and brimstone, where the beast and the false prophet are, and shall be tormented day and night for ever and ever.

REVELATION 20:11-15. THE GREAT WHITE THRONE JUDGMENT OF THE WICKED DEAD IS SURE. THOSE WHO REFUSED TO ACCEPT JESUS CHRIST AS THEIR LORD AND SAVIOUR WILL BE JUDGED. JESUS HIMSELF WILL BE THE JUDGE AND FINAL AUTHORITY – THOSE JUDGED CAN'T HIDE, POSTPONE, OR ESCAPE. – BY THEIR VERDICT (GUILTY) ETERNAL PUNISHMENT IS ASSURED. ALL THE EVIL DEEDS THEY COMMITTED DURING THEIR LIFETIME WILL BE ACCOUNTED FOR. NO PLACE TO RUN. NO PLACE TO HIDE. LET THOSE WHO ARE JUDGED HERE ABANDON ALL HOPE.

Revelation 20:11-15** And I saw a great white throne, and him that sat on it, from whose face the earth and the heaven fled away; and there was found no place for them. **12** And I saw the dead, small and great, stand before God; and the books were opened: and another book was opened, which is the book of life: and the dead were judged out of those things which were written in the books, according to their works. **13** And the sea gave up the dead which* *were in it; and death and hell delivered up the dead which were in them: and they were judged every man according to their works.* ***14 *And death and hell were cast into the lake of fire. This is the second death.* ***15*** *And whosoever was not found written in the book of life was cast into the lake of fire.*

PHILIPPIANS 2:5-11. IN THIS PASSAGE, PAUL INSTRUCTED THE SAINTS TO LET THEIR MINDS BE LIKE THAT OF JESUS. IN OTHER WORDS, LET THE MIND OF JESUS CONTROL THEIR LIVES.

NOTE IN VERSE 6 OF PHILIPPIANS 2 BELOW, CHRIST HAS ALWAYS BEEN GOD. HE WAS, IS, AND WILL FOREVER BE GOD. CO-EQUAL WITH GOD THE FATHER AND GOD THE HOLY SPIRIT. NOT THREE GODS, BUT A TRIUNE GOD. THREE IDENTITES, ONE GOD.

IN VERSES 7-8 OF PHILIPPIANS 2, HE DID NOT COME TO MAKE A REPUTATION. HE PUT ON THE FORM OF MAN AND BECAME A SERVANT FOR ONE PURPOSE, TO SAVE SINNERS LIKE YOU AND ME. HE PAID THE PRICE OF OUR REDEMPTION THROUGH HIS BLOOD AND OFFERED IT AS A FREE GIFT FOR THE TAKERS. WILL YOU RECEIVE THIS GIFT OR REJECT IT?

Philippians 2:5-11 *Let this mind be in you, which was also in Christ Jesus:* ***6*** *Who, being in the form of God,*

CHAPTER 2: THE GREAT WHITE THRONE JUDGMENT

*thought it not robbery to be equal with God: **7** But made himself of no reputation, and took upon him the form of a servant, and was made in the likeness of men: **8** And being found in fashion as a man, he humbled himself, and became obedient unto death, even the death of the cross. **9** Wherefore God also hath highly exalted him, and given him a name which is above every name: **10** That at the name of Jesus every knee should bow, of things in heaven, and things in earth, and things under the earth; **11** And that every tongue should confess that Jesus Christ is Lord, to the glory of God the Father.*

OBSERVE IN VERSES 9-11 OF PHILIPPIANS 2 ABOVE, THAT JESUS' RETURN WILL NOT BE AS A SERVANT; IT WILL BE AS <u>LORD OF LORDS</u> AND <u>KING OF KINGS</u>. EVERY KNEE <u>WILL</u> BOW BECAUSE HE <u>WILL</u> BE RECOGNIZED AS GOD THE SON. EVERY TONGUE <u>WILL</u> CONFESS THAT JESUS IS LORD. WITH THESE FACTS IN THE MINDS OF THOSE WHO WILL BE BOWING AT THE GREAT WHITE THRONE JUDGMENT, WHAT FEAR, WHAT REMORSE, WHAT <u>LOST</u> OPPORTUNITY WILL PLAGUE THEIR SOUL? NO PLACE TO RUN; NO PLACE TO HIDE. ONLY THE FIRE OF HELL AWAITS. ALL HOPE ABANDONED.

REVELATION 20:12. REVEALS THAT NO MATTER WHO YOU ARE ON THIS EARTH YOU <u>WILL NOT BE</u> EXEMPT. THE BOOKS CONTAIN A PERFECT RECORD OF <u>ALL</u> THINGS AND WORKS WHICH THE LOST PERSON HAS EVER COMMITTED. THE BOOK OF LIFE WILL <u>NOT</u> CONTAIN THE NAMES OF PEOPLE WHO REJECT JESUS. ALL THOSE AT THIS JUDGMENT ARE LOST. THEIR VERDICT IS GUILTY. ETERNITY AWAITS THEM IN THE LAKE OF FIRE.

> ***Revelation 20:12*** *And I saw the dead, small and great, stand before God; and the books were opened: and another book was opened, which is the book of life: and the dead were judged out of those things which were written in the books, according to their works.*

SINCE ALL THESE PEOPLE ARE LOST AND THEIR VERDICT IS SURE, WHY DO THEIR WORKS NEED TO BE CONSIDERED AT ALL? IT COULD ONLY BE TO DETERMINE THE QUANTITY AND GRAVITY OF THEIR SINS IN ORDER TO DETERMINE THEIR DEGREE OF PUNISHMENT. BUT <u>ALL WILL SUFFER HELL</u>.

LUKE 12:42-48. THE PARABLE OF THE DISOBEYING SERVANTS SHOWS WHO AND HOW THE UNSAVED WILL BE PUNISHED. THEY WILL GET ALL THAT THEY DESERVE. THIS PARABLE TEACHES THAT THERE WILL BE VARYING DEGREES OF PUNISHMENT IN

CHAPTER 2: THE GREAT WHITE THRONE JUDGMENT

HELL. TORMENT WILL NOT BE UNIFORM, BUT <u>ALL</u> WILL SUFFER HELL.

> ***Luke 12:42** And the Lord said, Who then is that faithful and wise steward, whom his lord shall make ruler over his household, to give them their portion of meat in due season? **43** Blessed is that servant, whom his lord when he cometh shall find so doing. **44** Of a truth I say unto you, that he will make him ruler over all that he hath. **45** But and if that servant say in his heart, My lord delayeth his coming; and shall begin to beat the menservants and maidens, and to eat and drink, and to be drunken; **46** The lord of that servant will come in a day when he looketh not for him, and at an hour when he is not aware, and will cut him in sunder, and will appoint him his portion with the unbelievers. **47** And that servant, which knew his lord's will, and prepared not himself, neither did according to his will, shall be beaten with many stripes. **48** But he that knew not, and did commit things worthy of stripes, shall be beaten with few stripes. For unto whomsoever much is given, of him shall be much required: and to whom men have committed much, of him they will ask the more.*

REVELATION 20:12-13. REVEALS THAT THE BODIES OF THE UNSAVED WILL AT THIS TIME UNITE WITH THEIR SOULS FROM HELL AND BE JUDGED AT THE GREAT WHITE THRONE JUDGMENT. THEY WILL BE JUDGED ACCORDING TO THEIR <u>WORKS.</u>

> *Revelation 20:12* And I saw the dead, small and great, stand before God; and the books were opened: and another book was opened, which is the book of life: and the dead were judged out of those things which were written in the books, according to their works. *13* And the sea gave up the dead which were in it; and death and hell delivered up the dead which were in them: and they were judged every man according to their works.

REVELATION 20:14. DEATH (BODIES) AND HELL (SOULS) WILL BE CAST INTO THE "LAKE OF FIRE." THIS IS THE SECOND DEATH, ETERNAL SEPARATION FROM GOD AND FROM ALL THOSE WHO ARE OR WILL BE SAVED. NO HOPE!

> *Revelation 20:14* And death and hell were cast into the lake of fire. This is the second death. *15* And whosoever was not found written in the book of life was cast into the lake of fire.

MARK 9:44, 48. THE LAKE OF FIRE EXHAUSTS HUMAN LANGUAGE TO DESCRIBE.

CHAPTER 2: THE GREAT WHITE THRONE JUDGMENT

IT IS A REAL PLACE THAT IS ETERNAL. IT WILL NEVER BE EXTENGUISHED:

> *Mark 9:44, 48* Where their worm dieth not, and the fire is not quenched.

MATTHEW 7:23, MATTHEW 8:12. AND IF YOU DO NOT KNOW, REALLY KNOW, JESUS, YOU WILL BE CAST OUT FROM HIS PRESENCE INTO OUTER DARKNESS.

> *Matthew 7:23* And then will I profess unto them, I never knew you: depart from me, ye that work iniquity.

> *Matthew 8:12* But the children of the kingdom shall be cast out into outer darkness: there shall be weeping and gnashing of teeth.

REVELATION 14:11. THE SMOKE OF THEIR TORMENT GOES UP FOREVER AND EVER.

> *Revelation 14:11* And the smoke of their torment ascendeth up for ever and ever: and they have no rest day nor night, who worship the beast and his image, and whosoever receiveth the mark of his name.

ALWAYS CONSCIOUS, EXPERIENCING UNRELENTING TORMENT DAY AFTER DAY;

YEAR AFTER YEAR; CENTURY AFTER CENTURY. IT IS FOR <u>ALL</u> ETERNITY.

MATTHEW 28:19-20. FOR YOU WHO ARE SAVED I SAY, "WHY, OH WHY, AREN'T WE CONCERNED WITH PEOPLE DYING IN THEIR SINS, AND MAKE THE GREAT COMMISSION A PRIORITY IN OUR LIVES?" IT IS A COMMANDMENT OF GOD TO <u>ALL</u> CHRISTIANS.

> *Matthew 28:19 Go ye therefore, and teach all nations, baptizing them in the name of the Father, and of the Son, and of the Holy Ghost: 20 Teaching them to observe all things whatsoever I have commanded you: and, lo, I am with you alway, even unto the end of the world. Amen.*

PSALM 126:5-6. IF WE WOULD APPLY THE FOLLOWING PROVERB TO OUR HEART WE WOULD TELL OTHERS ABOUT JESUS AND WHAT IT COST HIM TO SAVE OUR SOUL. THAT SHOULD BRING US TO UNSPEAKABLE JOY. NO ONE WILL REAP WITHOUT SOWING.

> *Psalm 126:5-6 They that sow in tears shall reap in joy. 6 He that goeth forth and weepeth, bearing precious seed, shall doubtless come again with rejoicing, bringing his sheaves with him.*

CHAPTER 2: THE GREAT WHITE THRONE JUDGMENT

JOHN 14:21, JOHN 15:8. JESUS SAID IN JOHN 14:15, "IF YOU LOVE ME, KEEP MY COMMANDMENTS." YOU CAN ONLY GO FORTH AND PRODUCE FRUIT BY OBEYING GOD. HE ALSO SAID, "HEREIN IS MY FATHER GLORIFIED, THAT YOU BEAR MUCH FRUIT."

> *John 14:21* He that hath my commandments, and keepeth them, he it is that loveth me: and he that loveth me shall be loved of my Father, and I will love him, and will manifest myself to him.
>
> *John 15:8* Herein is my Father glorified, that ye bear much fruit; so shall ye be my disciples.

ROMANS 12:1-2. PRESENTING OUR BODIES A LIVING SACRIFICE, HOLY, <u>ACCEPTABLE</u> TO GOD, IS OUR REASONABLE SERVICE. NOT TO DO SO MUST BE <u>UNACCEPTABLE</u>.

WE NEED TO JUDGE OURSELVES BEFORE IT IS TOO LATE.

> *Romans 12:1-2* I beseech you therefore, brethren, by the mercies of God, that ye present your bodies a living sacrifice, holy, acceptable unto God, which is your reasonable service. *2* And be not conformed to this world: but be ye transformed by the renewing of your mind, that ye may

prove what is that good, and acceptable, and perfect, will of God.

EZEKIEL 3:17-21; 33:7-8. MOST OF THE OLD TESTAMENT IS WRITTEN TO THE JEWS, BUT ALL SCRIPTURE HAS APPLICATION TO EVERYONE. WHEN WE MEET GOD, HOW MUCH BLOOD WILL BE DRIPPING FROM OUR HANDS? HOW MANY WILL SAY TO US "YOU DID NOT WARN ME! WHY? WHY?" ALL SAVED PEOPLE HAVE A RESPONSIBILITY AND COMMANDMENT FROM GOD TO WARN LOST PEOPLE OF THEIR COMING JUDGMENT AT "THE GREAT WHITE THRONE JUDGMENT" OF CHRIST.

***Ezekiel 3:17-21** Son of man, I have made thee a watchman unto the house of Israel: therefore hear the word at my mouth, and give them warning from me. **18** When I say unto the wicked, Thou shalt surely die; and thou givest him not warning, nor speakest to warn the wicked from his wicked way, to save his life; the same wicked man shall die in his iniquity; but his blood will I require at thine hand. **19** Yet if thou warn the wicked, and he turn not from his wickedness, nor from his wicked way, he shall die in his iniquity; but thou hast delivered thy soul. **20** Again, When a righteous man doth turn from his righteousness, and commit iniquity, and I lay a*

CHAPTER 2: THE GREAT WHITE THRONE JUDGMENT

stumblingblock before him, he shall die: because thou hast not given him warning, he shall die in his sin, and his righteousness which he hath done shall not be remembered; but his blood will I require at thine hand. ***21*** *Nevertheless if thou warn the righteous man, that the righteous sin not, and he doth not sin, he shall surely live, because he is warned; also thou hast delivered thy soul.*

Ezekiel 33:7-8 *So thou, O son of man, I have set thee a watchman unto the house of Israel; therefore thou shalt hear the word at my mouth, and warn them from me.* ***8*** *When I say unto the wicked, O wicked man, thou shalt surely die; if thou dost not speak to warn the wicked from his way, that wicked man shall die in his iniquity; but his blood will I require at thine hand.*

1 CORINTHIANS 6:9-10. BE NOT DECEIVED. THE GREAT WHITE THRONE JUDGMENT <u>WILL</u> OCCUR. SEEING OUR LOVED ONES AND EVEN STRANGERS TOSSED INTO THE LAKE OF FIRE BECAUSE OF OUR LACK OF CONCERN AND FAILURE TO WARN THEM WILL BE DEVASTATING. WE HAD BETTER WAKE UP.

1 Corinthians 6:9-10 *Know ye not that the unrighteous shall not inherit* *the kingdom of God? Be not deceived: neither fornicators, nor idolaters, nor adulterers, nor effeminate, nor abusers of themselves with mankind,* ***10*** *Nor thieves, nor covetous, nor drunkards, nor revilers, nor extortioners, shall inherit the kingdom of God.*

GOD GAVE US ALL A FREE CHOICE. WE CAN AVOID THE GREAT WHITE THRONE JUDGMENT. IF YOU HAVE NOT BEEN SAVED, REPENT OF YOUR SINS AND TRUST JESUS CHRIST NOW! TOMORROW NEVER COMES!

Joshua 24:15 *And if it seem evil unto you to serve the LORD,* ***choose you*** *this day whom ye will serve; whether the gods which your fathers served that were on the other side of the flood, or the gods of the Amorites, in whose land ye dwell: but as for me and my house, we will serve the LORD.*

CHAPTER 3
HELL

MANY PEOPLE TODAY DO NOT BELIEVE THERE IS A HELL. THEY SAY A LOVING GOD WOULD <u>NOT</u> SEND ANYONE TO SUCH AN AWFUL PLACE OF ETERNAL TORMENT. THE TRUTH IS GOD DID NOT CREATE HELL FOR PEOPLE. HE CREATED HELL FOR THE DEVIL AND HIS DEMONS. HE CREATED HEAVEN FOR PEOPLE. PEOPLE SEND THEMSELVES TO HELL BY REFUSING THE PAYMENT THAT JESUS MADE FOR THEIR SINS.

WHAT DOES THE BIBLE SAY? IS HELL <u>REAL</u>? <u>WHERE</u> IS HELL? <u>WHO</u> GOES THERE? <u>WHAT</u> IS IT <u>LIKE</u>? ARE THERE <u>DEGREES</u> OF <u>PUNISHMENT</u>? IS THERE <u>ANY</u> <u>HOPE</u> FOR THOSE IN HELL?

THE WORDS <u>SHEOL</u> IN THE OLD TESTAMENT AND <u>HADES</u> IN THE NEW TESTAMENT ARE TRANSLATED IN OUR BIBLE (KJV) AS <u>HELL</u>.

JESUS ALSO USES THE WORD <u>GEHENNA</u> TO SYMBOLICALLY DESCRIBE HELL. GEHENNA WAS A PLACE OUTSIDE THE GATES OF JERUSALEM WHERE THE CANAANITES SACRIFICED THEIR CHILDREN IN A FIRE THAT BURNED CONTINUOUSLY. DURING THE TIME OF JESUS IT WAS A GARBAGE DUMP WHERE <u>GARBAGE</u>, INCLUDING <u>DEAD</u> <u>BODIES</u> OF ANIMALS AND <u>EXECUTED</u> <u>CRIMINALS</u> WERE DISPOSED. THIS DUMP BURNED

CONTINUOUSLY. DOGS, FLIES, AND MAGGOTS WORKED THE FILTH. IT WAS SAID THAT AT NIGHT ONE COULD HEAR WILD DOGS HOWLING AS THEY FOUGHT OVER FOOD. CAN YOU IMAGINE THE SMELL OF THAT DUMP IF THE WIND BLEW TOWARD JERUSALEM? I REMEMBER MY EXPERIENCE IN MY HOMETOWN (MONTICELLO, FL). THE GARBAGE DUMP WAS A PLACE OF DEAD ANIMALS, MAGGOTS, FLIES, BUZZARDS, AND SOMETIMES DOGS. WE WENT THERE AS KIDS TO SHOOT BUZZARDS, BUT WE STAYED UPWIND DUE TO THE STINK.

MATTHEW 5:21, 22. IS HELL A REAL PLACE? JESUS SAID IT IS. THIS IS THE FIRST PLACE IN THE NEW TESTAMENT WHERE HELL IS MENTIONED. JESUS SAID HELL IS REAL AND IT IS A PLACE OF FIRE. WHOSOEVER MEANS WHO EVER. THAT INCLUDES YOU AND ME. RACA MEANS EMPTY HEADED OR SENSELESS. FOOL HERE MEANS BLOCKHEAD OR STUPID. GOD'S MORAL LAW SAYS LOVE YOUR NEIGHBOR AS YOURSELF, AND DON'T BE ANGRY WITH YOUR BROTHER WITHOUT A CAUSE. IF YOU DO YOU WILL BE IN DANGER OF JUDGMENT. IN OTHER WORDS, DON'T JUMP TO JUDGMENT. CALLING A PERSON A FOOL INDICATES HATE IN OUR OWN HEART. IT ALSO SHOWS THAT THE PERSON WE ARE ADDRESSING IS, BY US, DESPISED, HATED, AND NOT LOVED. THESE THINGS REFLECT UNFAVORABLY ON OUR OWN MORALS AND PUTS US IN DANGER OF THE FIRE OF HELL.

CHAPTER 3: HELL

Matthew 5:21-22. Ye have heard that it was said by them of old time, Thou shalt not kill; and whosoever shall kill shall be in danger of the judgment: **22** But I say unto you, That whosoever is angry with his brother without a cause shall be in danger of the judgment: and whosoever shall say to his brother, Raca, shall be in danger of the council: but whosoever shall say, Thou fool, shall be in danger of hell fire.

LUKE 16:19-31. JESUS TAUGHT THAT HELL IS A REAL PLACE. HE DESCRIBED IT BY THE FOLLOWING ACCOUNT. THE RICH MAN DIED IN HIS SINS AS AN UNREPENTANT SINNER. HE RECEIVED HIS JUST PUNISHMENT. HE WAS IN TORMENTS. HE PLEADED FOR JUST A WET FINGER TO COOL HIS TONGUE. (TOO LATE.) HE HAD COMPASSION FOR HIS FIVE BROTHERS. "TORMENT" IN THE GREEK MEANS GOING TO THE BOTTOM, LIKE A BLACK SILICEOUS STONE USED TO DETERMINE THE PURITY OF GOLD, SILVER, AND OTHER METALS. METAPHORICALLY IT MEANS A TRIAL BY TORTURE. JESUS SAID IN A SENSE, IF YOU WON'T HEAR MOSES AND THE PROPHETS (THE OLD TESTAMENT SAINTS) YOU WON'T BE PERSUADED <u>FOR ANY REASON</u>. HOW MUCH GREATER WILL BE YOUR LACK OF PERSUASION, IF YOU WON'T HEAR JESUS IN

ARE YOU READY?

THE NEW TESTAMENT. YOU <u>WILL</u> END UP IN THE SAME CONDITION AS THE RICH MAN, TORTURED FOR ALL ETERNITY. JESUS WARNS US MANY TIMES IN HIS HOLY WORD, BUT THIS DESCRIPTION SHOULD RUN CHILLS OF FEAR UP OUR SPINE.

Luke 16:19-31 There was a certain rich man, which was clothed in purple and fine linen, and fared sumptuously every day: 20 And there was a certain beggar named Lazarus, which was laid at his gate, full of sores, 21 And desiring to be fed with the crumbs which fell from the rich man's table: moreover the dogs came and licked his sores. 22 And it came to pass, that the beggar died, and was carried by the angels into Abraham's bosom: the rich man also died, and was buried; 23 And in hell he lift up his eyes, being in torments, and seeth Abraham afar off, and Lazarus in his bosom. 24 And he cried and said, Father Abraham, have mercy on me, and send Lazarus, that he may dip the tip of his finger in water, and cool my tongue; for I am tormented in this flame. 25 But Abraham said, Son, remember that thou in thy lifetime receivedst thy good things, and likewise Lazarus evil things: but now he is comforted, and thou art tormented. 26 And beside all this,

CHAPTER 3: HELL

between us and you there is a great gulf fixed: so that they which would pass from hence to you cannot; neither can they pass to us, that would come from thence. ***27*** *Then he said, I pray thee therefore, father, that thou wouldest send him to my father's house:* ***28*** *For I have five brethren; that he may testify unto them, lest they also come into this place of torment.* ***29*** *Abraham saith unto him, They have Moses and the prophets; let them hear them.* ***30*** *And he said, Nay, father Abraham: but if one went unto them from the dead, they will repent.* ***31*** *And he said unto him, If they hear not Moses and the prophets, neither will they be persuaded, though one rose from the dead.*

REVELATION 1:18, PSALM 119:89. JESUS HAS TOTAL AND COMPLETE AUTHORITY OVER ALL THINGS VISIBLE AND INVISIBLE IN THE ENTIRE UNIVERSE. HE HAS THE KEYS TO HELL AND OF DEATH. HE CAN OPEN AND NO ONE CAN SHUT. HE CAN SHUT AND NO ONE CAN OPEN. HE IS THE JUDGE FROM WHICH NO ONE CAN APPEAL AND NO ONE CAN ESCAPE. JESUS SAID HELL IS REAL, AND HIS WORD IS FOREVER SETTLED IN HEAVEN.

> **Revelation 1:18** I am he that liveth, and was dead; and, behold, I am alive for evermore, Amen; and have the keys of hell and of death.
>
> **Psalm 119:89** For ever, O LORD, thy word is settled in heaven.

WHEN WAS HELL CREATED?

GENESIS 1:1,27; 2:8. IN THE BEGINNING GOD CREATED THE HEAVEN AND THE EARTH. WE ARE <u>NOT</u> TOLD WHEN HELL WAS CREATED, BUT WE KNOW GOD CREATED HEAVEN AND EARTH IN SIX DAYS. WHEN MAN WAS CREATED HE WAS PLACED IN A PERFECT ENVIRONMENT WITH NO EXISTING SIN. THERE WOULD BE NO NEED FOR HELL EXCEPT FOR SATAN AND HIS ANGELS. NO ONE KNOWS WHEN HELL WAS CREATED, BUT WE DO KNOW WHY.

> **Genesis 1:1** In the beginning God created the heaven and the earth.
> **Genesis 1:27** So God created man in his own image, in the image of God created he him; male and female created he them.
> **Genesis 2:8** And the LORD God planted a garden eastward in Eden; and there he put the man whom he had formed.

MATTHEW 25:41. THE BIBLE CLEARLY TEACHES US THAT HELL WAS CREATED FOR

CHAPTER 3: HELL

THE "DEVIL AND HIS ANGELS," <u>NOT</u> PEOPLE. GOD CREATED <u>HEAVEN</u> FOR PEOPLE, BUT HE WARNED THAT "YE WILL NOT COME TO ME THAT YOU MIGHT HAVE LIFE." PEOPLE CHOOSE TO GO TO HELL BY REJECTING JESUS.

> *Matthew 25:41 Then shall he say also unto them on the left hand, Depart from me, ye cursed, into everlasting fire, prepared for the devil and his angels:*

ISAIAH 14:12-15. SATAN WAS PERFECT UNTIL INIQUITY WAS FOUND IN HIM. HE WANTED TO BE ABOVE GOD. HE REBELLED AGAINST GOD AND CAUSED MANY ANGELS TO FOLLOW HIM. SOME OF THESE WERE DELIVERED INTO "CHAINS OF DARKNESS." WHERE IS THIS PLACE OF CHAINS OF DARKNESS?

> *Isaiah 14:12-15 How art thou fallen from heaven, O Lucifer, son of the morning! how art thou cut down to the ground, which didst weaken the nations! 13 For thou hast said in thine heart, I will ascend into heaven, I will exalt my throne above the stars of God: I will sit also upon the mount of the congregation, in the sides of the north: 14 I will ascend above the heights of the clouds; I will be like the most High. 15 Yet thou shalt be*

brought down to hell, to the sides of the pit.

GENESIS 3:1, 3, 6. SINCE <u>SATAN</u> TEMPTED EVE IN THE GARDEN OF EDEN AND CAUSED ADAM TO SIN, HELL WOULD HAVE HAD TO BE IN EXISTANCE TO HOUSE THE <u>FIRST</u> PERSON WHO DIED <u>IN</u> THEIR SINS (WHOEVER THAT WAS). GOD'S FOREKNOWLEDGE UNDOUBTEDLY KNEW HELL WAS NEEDED. (HEAVEN AND EARTH WERE CREATED IN SIX DAYS.)

> ***Genesis 3:1*** *Now the serpent was more subtil than any beast of the field which the LORD God had made. And he said unto the woman, Yea, hath God said, Ye shall not eat of every tree of the garden?* ***Genesis 3:3*** *But of the fruit of the tree which is in the midst of the garden, God hath said, Ye shall not eat of it, neither shall ye touch it, lest ye die.* ***Genesis 3:6*** *And when the woman saw that the tree was good for food, and that it was pleasant to the eyes, and a tree to be desired to make one wise, she took of the fruit thereof, and did eat, and gave also unto her husband with her; and he did eat.*

WHERE IS HELL?

EPHESIANS 4:8-10. JESUS DESCENDED INTO THE LOWER PARTS OF THE EARTH. THE

CHAPTER 3: HELL

LOWER PARTS MUST REFER TO THE CENTER OF THE EARTH.

> *Ephesians 4:8 Wherefore he saith, When he ascended up on high, he led captivity captive, and gave gifts unto men. 9 (Now that he ascended, what is it but that he also descended first into the lower parts of the earth? 10 He that descended is the same also that ascended up far above all heavens, that he might fill all things.)*

NUMBERS 16:28-33, ISAIAH 14:9, ISAIAH 14:15, EZEKIEL 26:20. PIT HERE IS TRANSLATED FROM THE HEBREW WORD SHEOL WHICH IS HELL. BEFORE THE DEATH OF JESUS HELL HAD TWO COMPARTMENTS SEPARATED BY A GREAT GULF AS WE SAW IN LUKE 16:19-31. ON ONE SIDE WAS PARADISE WHERE THE OLD TESTAMENT SAINTS WERE, ON THE OTHER SIDE WAS WHAT WE CALL HELL, THE PLACE OF TORMENT. JESUS LED THE SAINTS IN THE PARADISE SECTION WITH HIM INTO HEAVEN AFTER HIS DEATH AND BEFORE HIS RESURRECTION.

> *Numbers 16:28-33 And Moses said, Hereby ye shall know that the LORD hath sent me to do all these works; for I have not done them of mine own mind. 29 If these men die the common death of all men, or if they be visited after the visitation of all*

men; then the LORD hath not sent me. **30** But if the LORD make a new thing, and the earth open her mouth, and swallow them up, with all that appertain unto them, and they go down quick into the pit; then ye shall understand that these men have provoked the LORD. **31** And it came to pass, as he had made an end of speaking all these words, that the ground clave asunder that was under them: **32** And the earth opened her mouth, and swallowed them up, and their houses, and all the men that appertained unto Korah, and all their goods. **33** They, and all that appertained to them, went down alive into the pit, and the earth closed upon them: and they perished from among the congregation.

Isaiah 14:9 Hell from beneath is moved for thee to meet thee at thy coming: it stirreth up the dead for thee, even all the chief ones of the earth; it hath raised up from their thrones all the kings of the nations.

Isaiah 14:15 Yet thou shalt be brought down to hell, to the sides of the pit.

Ezekiel 26:20 When I shall bring thee down with them that descend into the pit, with the people of old

CHAPTER 3: HELL

time, and shall set thee in the low parts of the earth, in places desolate of old, with them that go down to the pit, that thou be not inhabited; and I shall set glory in the land of the living;

PSALM 16:9, 10, LUKE 23:43. HELL HERE IS THE PARADISE COMPARTMENT.

Psalm 16:9-10 *Therefore my heart is glad, and my glory rejoiceth: my flesh also shall rest in hope.* ***10*** *For thou wilt not leave my soul in hell; neither wilt thou suffer thine Holy One to see corruption.*

Luke 23:43 *And Jesus said unto him, Verily I say unto thee, To day shalt thou be with me in paradise.*

MATTHEW 12:38-40. JESUS HIMSELF DECLARED THAT HE WOULD DESCEND INTO THE "HEART OF THE EARTH," AGAIN, THE PARADISE SECTION OF HELL. HELL IS A REAL PLACE AND IT IS IN THE CENTER OF THE EARTH.

Matthew 12:38-40 *Then certain of the scribes and of the Pharisees answered, saying, Master, we would see a sign from thee.* ***39*** *But he answered and said unto them, An evil and adulterous generation seeketh after a sign; and there shall no sign* *be given to it, but the sign of the prophet Jonas:* **40** *For as Jonas was three days and three nights in the whale's belly; so shall the Son of man be three days and three nights in the heart of the earth.*

HOW LONG WILL THE LOST BE IN HELL AND WHAT IS THE PUNISHMENT?

MATTHEW 25:41. JESUS SAID HELL IS A PLACE OF "<u>EVERLASTING FIRE</u>." LUKE 16 SAYS IT IS A PLACE OF "<u>TORMENTS</u>" (PLURAL), A PLACE OF <u>NO WATER</u>.

Matthew 25:41 Then shall he say also unto them on the left hand, Depart from me, ye cursed, into everlasting fire, prepared for the devil and his angels:

MATTHEW 25:46. JESUS SAID HELL IS "<u>EVERLASTING PUNISHMENT</u>."

Matthew 25:46 And these shall go away into everlasting punishment: but the righteous into life eternal.

REVELATION 14:9-11. LOST PEOPLE WILL BE TORMENTED "WITH FIRE AND BRIMSTONE" "DAY AND NIGHT" "FOREVER AND EVER." THEY WILL NEVER HAVE ANY REST. THERE IS NO ESCAPE. ETERNAL PUNISHMENT.

CHAPTER 3: HELL

***Revelation 14:9-11** And the third angel followed them, saying with a loud voice, If any man worship the beast and his image, and receive his mark in his forehead, or in his hand,* **10** *The same shall drink of the wine of the wrath of God, which is poured out without mixture into the cup of his indignation; and he shall be tormented with fire and brimstone in the presence of the holy angels, and in the presence of the Lamb:* **11** *And the smoke of their torment ascendeth up for ever and ever: and they have no rest day nor night, who worship the beast and his image, and whosoever receiveth the mark of his name.*

REVELATION 20:11-15. THOSE WHOSE NAME WAS NOT FOUND IN THE BOOK OF LIFE WERE CAST INTO THE LAKE OF FIRE—LOST PEOPLE...THOSE WHO REJECTED CHRIST'S PAYMENT FOR THEIR SINS. HELL IS A REAL PLACE; AN AWFUL PLACE OF TORMENT, AND AN ETERNAL PLACE. NO ESCAPE.

Revelation 20:11-15** And I saw a great white throne, and him that sat on it, from whose face the earth and the heaven fled away; and there was found no place for them.* **12** *And I saw the dead, small and great, stand* *before God; and the books were opened: and another book was opened, which is the book of life: and the dead were judged out of those things which were written in the books, according to their works.* ***13 *And the sea gave up the dead which were in it; and death and hell delivered up the dead which were in them: and they were judged every man according to their works.* ***14*** *And death and hell were cast into the lake of fire. This is the second death.* ***15*** *And whosoever was not found written in the book of life was cast into the lake of fire.*

1 PETER 5:8. CAN YOU PICTURE YOURSELF FAR OUT INTO A JUNGLE WITH NO WEAPON AND WITH A HUNGRY, ROARING LION STALKING YOU? YOU KNOW WHAT WOULD HAPPEN? YOU WOULD BE DEVOURED. NO PLACE TO RUN. NO PLACE TO HIDE. NOW PICTURE THE <u>DEVIL</u> STALKING YOU JUST LIKE THE LION, BUT WITH A BIG DIFFERENCE. THE DEVIL IS THE <u>PRINCE AND POWER OF THE AIR</u>. YOU CAN'T SEE HIM. HE HAS <u>EXTREME POWER</u>. HE IS VERY INTELLIGENT. HE HAS <u>THOUSANDS OF DEMONS</u> WHO DO HIS WILL. <u>HE WILL NOT STOP</u>! HE JUST KEEPS ON COMING! <u>SATAN DESIRES OUR SOUL MORE</u> THAN THE LION DESIRES HIS SUPPER. WE <u>HAD</u> BETTER BE <u>SOBER AND VIGILANT</u> 24 HOURS A DAY, 7

CHAPTER 3: HELL

DAYS PER WEEK. WE <u>HAD</u> BETTER <u>PUT ON THE WHOLE ARMOR OF GOD</u> (EPHESIANS 6:11) IF WE WANT TO <u>STAND</u> AGAINST THE ONSLAUGHT OF THE DEVIL. WE CAN'T DO IT IN OUR OWN POWER. THE DEVIL IS DETERMINED TO SEE ALL OF US <u>BURN IN HELL</u>. UNTIL WE GET SAVED HE ALREADY HAS US IN HIS CLAWS.

> ***1 Peter 5:8*** *Be sober, be vigilant; because your adversary the devil, as a roaring lion, walketh about, seeking whom he may devour:*

HELL IS A REAL PLACE. IT IS A PLACE OF EVERLASTING TORMENTS. THE DEVIL WANTS OUR SOULS. HE IS THE GREAT DECEIVER. WE MUST BE SOBER AND VIGILANT TO HIS DECEPTIVE DEVICES.

ARE THERE DIFFERENT DEGREES OF PUNISHMENT IN HELL?

MATTHEW 16:27. JESUS TOLD HIS <u>DISCIPLES</u> THAT HE WILL COME AGAIN AND "<u>REWARD</u>" EVERY MAN <u>ACCORDING TO HIS WORKS</u>. THE REWARDS OF A CHRISTIAN ARE <u>BASED ON THEIR WORKS</u>. ONE MIGHT THINK THAT REWARDS ARE EARNED BY THE QUANTITY AND QUALITY OF WORKS. BUT ARE THEY? WOULDN'T THIS GIVE AN UNFAIR ADVANTAGE TO THE SUPER RICH?

> ***Matthew 16:27*** *For the Son of man shall come in the glory of his Father*

with his angels; and then he shall reward every man according to his works.

MARK 12:41-44. JESUS SAID THAT ALL THAT THE PEOPLE DID WAS TO CAST IN OF THEIR ABUNDANCE, BUT THE WIDOW LADY CAST IN MORE THAN <u>THEY ALL</u>. SHE CAST IN HER LIVING, TWO MITES. (TAKES ABOUT 4 TO MAKE 1 CENT.) SHE MADE A <u>HUGE SACRIFICE</u> BASED ON HER <u>ABILITY</u>. SHE GAVE IT ALL. JESUS SEEING THIS SAID SHE CAST IN <u>MORE THAN THEY ALL</u>. MORE THAN ALL THE OTHERS PUT TOGETHER. <u>REWARDS ARE BASED ON ABILITY AND SACRIFICE</u>. GOD'S <u>JUSTICE</u> DEMANDS THAT THE WIDOW LADY RECEIVE THE GREATER REWARD. IF REWARDS ARE JUDGED WOULDN'T A JUST GOD PRONOUNCE DEGREES OF PUNISHMENT IN HELL?

*Mark 12:41-44 And Jesus sat over against the treasury, and beheld how the people cast money into the treasury: and many that were rich cast in much. **42** And there came a certain poor widow, and she threw in two mites, which make a farthing. **43** And he called unto him his disciples, and saith unto them, Verily I say unto you, That this poor widow hath cast more in, than all they which have cast into the treasury: **44** For all they did cast in of their abundance; but she of*

CHAPTER 3: HELL

her want did cast in all that she had, even all her living.

DEUTERONOMY 32:4. GOD IS THE <u>ROCK</u>. HIS WAYS ARE <u>PERFECT</u>, <u>ALL</u> HIS WAYS ARE <u>JUDGMENT</u>, A GOD OF <u>TRUTH</u> WITHOUT <u>INIQUITY</u>, <u>JUST</u> AND <u>RIGHT</u> IS <u>HE</u>. WE NEED TO KEEP THAT IN OUR MIND. GOD IS JUST. HE WILL DO <u>NO</u> INJUSTICE.

***Deuteronomy 32:4** He is the Rock, his work is perfect: for all his ways are judgment: a God of truth and without iniquity, just and right is he.*

NOW THE CERTAINTY ARISES THAT IF GOD IS JUST, SIN MUST BE PUNISHED. IF SO, ARE THERE DEGREES OF PUNISHMENT IN HELL? IT SEEMS THAT MORE AND MORE MAN'S JUSTICE SYSTEM IS BASED ON ONE'S ENVIRONMENT AND REHABILITATION. NOT GOD'S! HIS JUSTICE SYSTEM IS BASED ON REWARDING GOOD AND PUNISHING SIN. THE ONLY CURE OF OUR SIN IS THE BLOOD OF JESUS CHRIST. THE WAGES OF SIN IS DEATH, THE SECOND DEATH IN THE LAKE OF FIRE.

REVELATION 20:11-15. PEOPLE WHO REJECT THE REDEEMING BLOOD OF JESUS WILL BE "<u>JUDGED ACCORDING TO THEIR WORKS.</u>" BUT THEY <u>ALL</u> WILL BE CAST INTO THE LAKE OF FIRE.

Revelation 20:11-15 *And I saw a great white throne, and him that sat on it, from whose face the earth and the heaven fled away; and there was found no place for them.* ***12*** *And I saw the dead, small and great, stand before God; and the books were opened: and another book was opened, which is the book of life: and the dead were judged out of those things which were written in the books, according to their works.* ***13*** *And the sea gave up the dead which were in it; and death and hell delivered up the dead which were in them: and they were judged every man according to their works.* ***14*** *And death and hell were cast into the lake of fire. This is the second death.* ***15*** *And whosoever was not found written in the book of life was cast into the lake of fire.*

THE BIBLE TEACHES, "WHATSOEVER A MAN SOWETH, THAT SHALL HE ALSO REAP," (GALATIANS 6:7). SOW LITTLE, REAP LITTLE; SOW A LOT, REAP A LOT.

JOHN 19:10-11. WHEN PILATE HEARD THAT JESUS CLAIMED TO BE THE "SON OF GOD" HE BECAME AFRAID. REMEMBER THAT HE HAD ALREADY BEEN WARNED BY HIS WIFE WHO TOLD HIM TO HAVE <u>NOTHING</u> TO DO WITH THIS JUST MAN. PILATE SAID TO JESUS, "I HAVE THE POWER TO CRUCIFY

CHAPTER 3: HELL

THEE." CHRIST REMINDS HIM THAT ALL HIS AUTHORITY WAS GIVEN HIM BY GOD AND THAT THOSE WHO DELIVERED HIM HAD THE "<u>GREATER SIN.</u>" WE LIKE TO THINK OF SIN AS A <u>UNIT</u> WHEN IT COMES TO PUNISHMENT IN HELL, BUT JESUS DECLARES THE PRIESTS AND THEIR FOLLOWERS <u>HAD</u> THE <u>GREATER SIN</u>. THEY WILL RECEIVE THE GREATER PUNISHMENT.

> *John 19:10-11* Then saith Pilate unto him, Speakest thou not unto me? knowest thou not that I have power to crucify thee, and have power to release thee? *11* Jesus answered, Thou couldest have no power at all against me, except it were given thee from above: therefore he that delivered me unto thee hath the greater sin.

MATTHEW 23:13-14. THESE HYPOCRITES SHUT UP THE KINGDOM OF HEAVEN BY PUTTING STUMBLING BLOCKS IN THE WAY OF A SINNER COMING TO REPENTANCE. YE DEVOUR WIDOWS HOUSES, WHILE MAKING A SHOW OF BEING RELIGIOUS. THESE PHARISEES WHO ARE HYPOCRITES <u>WILL RECEIVE THE</u> <u>GREATER DAMNATION</u>, THAT IS A MORE SEVERE SENTENCE, A GREATER PUNISHMENT IN HELL.

> *Matthew 23:13-14* But woe unto you, scribes and Pharisees, hypocrites! for ye shut up the

> *kingdom of heaven against men: for ye neither go in yourselves, neither suffer ye them that are entering to go in. **14** Woe unto you, scribes and Pharisees, hypocrites! for ye devour widows' houses, and for a pretence make long prayer: therefore ye shall receive the greater damnation.*

JAMES 1:19-20. WE ARE COMMANDED TO BE SWIFT TO HEAR, SLOW TO SPEAK, AND SLOW TO WRATH. THE PROBLEM IS TOO MUCH TALKING AND NOT ENOUGH LISTENING. NO ONE CAN TELL US ANYTHING. WE KNOW IT ALL.

> ***James 1:19-20** Wherefore, my beloved brethren, let every man be swift to hear, slow to speak, slow to wrath: **20** For the wrath of man worketh not the righteousness of God.*

JAMES 3:1. HAVING TOO MANY MASTERS (OR TEACHERS) IS LIKE HAVING MORE SUPERVISORS THAN LABORERS. JAMES TELLS THOSE WHO LEAD TO EXAMINE THEIR MOTIVES. ARE THEY OBEYING GOD OR SEEKING SELF GRATIFICATION, OR MONEY? <u>GREATER</u> PUNISHMENT IN HELL COULD BE THE RESULT OF EVIL MOTIVES, AND LESSER PUNISHMENT FOR THOSE WHO LEARN RIGHT AND DO RIGHT.

CHAPTER 3: HELL

James 3:1 My brethren, be not many masters, knowing that we shall receive the greater condemnation.

MATTHEW 11:20-24. JESUS TAUGHT VERY CLEARLY THAT THOSE WITH OPPORTUNITY WILL BE JUDGED MORE HARSHLY THAN THOSE WHO HAVE LESS OPPORTUNITY AND LESS TRUTH. KEEP IN MIND THAT JESUS WALKED, TAUGHT, AND PERFORMED MANY MIRACLES IN CAPERNAUM, BUT NOT IN SODOM. AFTER LEAVING NAZARETH JESUS MADE CAPERNAUM HIS HOME BASE. YET THEY WOULD NOT REPENT. THEY CONTINUED IN SIN. THEIR JUDGMENT WOULD BE MORE SEVERE.

Matthew 11:20-24 Then began he to upbraid the cities wherein most of his mighty works were done, because they repented not: 21 Woe unto thee, Chorazin! woe unto thee, Bethsaida! for if the mighty works, which were done in you, had been done in Tyre and Sidon, they would have repented long ago in sackcloth and ashes. 22 But I say unto you, It shall be more tolerable for Tyre and Sidon at the day of judgment, than for you. 23 And thou, Capernaum, which art exalted unto heaven, shalt be brought down to hell: for if the mighty works, which have been done in thee, had been done in Sodom, it would have remained until this day. **24** But I say unto you, That it shall be more tolerable for the land of Sodom in the day of judgment, than for thee.*

LUKE 12:47-48. JESUS CLEARLY TAUGHT THAT THOSE WHO KNOW GOD'S WILL BUT REFUSE TO DO HIS WILL WILL BE PUNISHED <u>MORE</u> THAN THOSE WHO HAVE NOT RECEIVED AS MUCH KNOWLEDGE OR UNDERSTANDING. TO WHOM MUCH IS GIVEN, MUCH WILL BE REQUIRED. THAT'S A SOBERING TRUTH THAT SHOULD MAKE US ALL QUIVER.

***Luke 12:47-48** And that servant, which knew his lord's will, and prepared not himself, neither did according to his will, shall be beaten with many stripes. **48** But he that knew not, and did commit things worthy of stripes, shall be beaten with few stripes. For unto whomsoever much is given, of him shall be much required: and to whom men have committed much, of him they will ask the more.*

KEEP IN MIND THAT IT IS GOD'S WILL THAT ALL BE SAVED. WHAT ABOUT A PERSON WHO HAS NEVER HEARD THE GOSPEL OF JESUS CHRIST? WOULD A JUST GOD PUNISH HIM?

CHAPTER 3: HELL

ROMANS 2:12-15. GOD REVEALS HIMSELF IN ALL CREATION. HE GAVE MAN A "<u>CONSCIENCE</u>," A "<u>FREE WILL</u>," AND THE ABILITY TO KNOW RIGHT FROM WRONG. HE SAID MAN IS <u>WITHOUT EXCUSE</u>.

Romans 2:12-15 For as many as have sinned without law shall also perish without law: and as many as have sinned in the law shall be judged by the law; **13** *(For not the hearers of the law are just before God, but the doers of the law shall be justified.* **14** *For when the Gentiles, which have not the law, do by nature the things contained in the law, these, having not the law, are a law unto themselves:* **15** *Which shew the work of the law written in their hearts, their conscience also bearing witness, and their thoughts the mean while accusing or else excusing one another;)*

JOHN 1:9. JOHN THE BAPTIST TESTIFIED THAT JESUS WAS THE "<u>TRUE LIGHT</u>" WHICH LIGHTETH <u>EVERY MAN</u> THAT COMETH INTO THE WORLD. JESUS IS THE LIGHT FOR EVERY MAN, EVEN TO THOSE WHO HAVE NEVER HEARD HIS NAME. THEIR LIGHT IS GOD'S CREATION AND THEIR CONSCIENCE BEARS WITNESS TO THE FACT THAT GOD IS REAL. WHAT WE DO WITH THE "LIGHT" IS UP TO US. ONE COULD ASK, HOW

COULD ANYONE GET SAVED WITHOUT HEARING ABOUT JESUS? OUR PROBLEM IS WE PUT GOD'S ABILITY IN A BOX AND IMAGINE IT CAN'T GET OUT. GOD CAN DO ANYTHING! HE SAID SEEK AND YOU WILL FIND, KNOCK AND IT WILL BE OPENED TO YOU. GOD CAN GET THE GOSPEL TO ANYONE ANYWHERE OR GET THAT PERSON TO THE GOSPEL. I REMEMBER EITHER HEARING OR READING A STORY OF A NATIVE CHIEF WHO, OBSERVING THE HEAVENS, DETERMINED THERE MUST BE A GOD. HIS DESIRE AND PRAYER WAS TO KNOW HIM. HE HAD A DREAM THAT A GREAT WHITE SHIP WOULD COME AND SOMEONE ON THAT SHIP WOULD REVEAL GOD. HE SENT A RUNNER TO THE COAST WHO OBSERVED A WHITE (RED CROSS) SHIP. HE LET HIS REQUEST BE KNOWN AND A MISSIONARY ON THE SHIP HEARD IT. THE MISSIONARY RETURNED TO THE VILLAGE WITH THE RUNNER AND PREACHED THE GOSPEL OF JESUS CHRIST. THE CHIEF AND MOST OF THE VILLAGE RECEIVED CHRIST AS THEIR SAVIOUR. WITH GOD ALL THINGS ARE POSSIBLE. NEITHER GOD NOR HIS ABILITY IS IN A BOX. THE AMOUNT OF LIGHT OR TRUTH THAT AMERICANS HAVE WOULD LIGHT UP THE UNIVERSE. YET OUR PEOPLE AND OUR NATION ARE GROWING DARKER AND DARKER. IF WE AS INDIVIDUALS DON'T REPENT AND START OBEYING GOD, I BELIEVE OUR CHILDREN COULD SOON BE IN TOTAL DARKNESS.

CHAPTER 3: HELL

John 1:9 That was the true Light, which lighteth every man that cometh into the world.

LUKE 16:19-31. TWO PEOPLE ARE DESCRIBED IN THIS SCRIPTURE. ONE A RICH MAN WHO HAD PLENTY. THE OTHER A BEGGAR WHO ONLY WANTED THE CRUMBS FROM THE RICH MAN'S TABLE. THEY BOTH DIED. ONE WENT TO HELL, THE OTHER TO PARADISE. THE RICH MAN WENT TO HELL, <u>NOT</u> BECAUSE HE WAS RICH, BUT BECAUSE HE WAS A SINNER WHO DID NOT HAVE FAITH IN GOD. A SINNER JUST LIKE YOU AND ME. THE BEGGAR WENT TO PARADISE, <u>NOT</u> BECAUSE HE WAS A GOOD MAN WHO HAD NOTHING, BUT BECAUSE HE HAD FAITH IN GOD.

Luke 16:19-31 There was a certain rich man, which was clothed in purple and fine linen, and fared sumptuously every day: 20 And there was a certain beggar named Lazarus, which was laid at his gate, full of sores, 21 And desiring to be fed with the crumbs which fell from the rich man's table: moreover the dogs came and licked his sores. 22 And it came to pass, that the beggar died, and was carried by the angels into Abraham's bosom: the rich man also died, and was buried; 23 And in hell he lift up his eyes, being in torments, and seeth Abraham afar off, and Lazarus in his bosom. **24** And he cried and said, Father Abraham, have mercy on me, and send Lazarus, that he may dip the tip of his finger in water, and cool my tongue; for I am tormented in this flame. **25** But Abraham said, Son, remember that thou in thy lifetime receivedst thy good things, and likewise Lazarus evil things: but now he is comforted, and thou art tormented. **26** And beside all this, between us and you there is a great gulf fixed: so that they which would pass from hence to you cannot; neither can they pass to us, that would come from thence. **27** Then he said, I pray thee therefore, father, that thou wouldest send him to my father's house: **28** For I have five brethren; that he may testify unto them, lest they also come into this place of torment. **29** Abraham saith unto him, They have Moses and the prophets; let them hear them. **30** And he said, Nay, father Abraham: but if one went unto them from the dead, they will repent. **31** And he said unto him, If they hear not Moses and the prophets, neither will they be persuaded, though one rose from the dead.

OUR GOD, WHO IS PERFECTLY JUST, PUNISHES SIN BUT OFFERS US AN ALTERNATIVE. HE WILL FORGIVE OUR SINS

CHAPTER 3: HELL

JUST LIKE HE DID THE BEGGAR <u>IF</u> WE PUT OUR TRUST AND FAITH IN HIM. ONLY A FOOL SAYS IN HIS HEART "THERE IS NO GOD." LOOK BACK AT LUKE 16. OUT OF ALL THE SINS COMMITTED BY THE RICH MAN WHICH ONE DID JESUS DESCRIBE? LACK OF <u>COMPASSION</u>! HE FAILED TO CONSIDER THE BEGGAR AT HIS GATE EVEN THOUGH HE HAD ALL THE MEANS TO HELP HIM. TODAY WITH MODERN MEANS OF COMMUNICATION OUR "GATE" IS THE ENTIRE WORLD, FROM OUR CLOSEST NEIGHBOR TO THE FARTHEST POINT ON EARTH. HUNGRY PEOPLE JUST LIKE THE BEGGAR ARE EVERYWHERE. MORE IMPORTANTLY, LOST PEOPLE ARE ON THEIR WAY TO A FIERY HELL. THEY ARE HUNGRY FOR THE GOSPEL.

NOW THINK ABOUT A <u>MODERN-DAY RICH</u> MAN. ONE WHO HAS A HOME, CAR, JOB, FOOD ON THE TABLE, CLOTHES ON HIS BACK, TELEPHONE, TELEVISION, AND CLEAN WATER. ONE WHOM THE SCRAPS FROM HIS TABLE AND FOOD NOT EATEN COULD PROBABLY FEED AT LEAST ONE OTHER PERSON. COMPARED TO THE REST OF THE WORLD THAT PERSON IS RICH. COMPARE THAT PERSON TO THE RICH MAN'S WEALTH IN LUKE 16. WHO DO YOU THINK IS THE RICHEST? HIM OR YOU? WHAT DO YOU THINK ABOUT <u>THIS</u> MODERN DAY RICH MAN? I THINK I KNOW. WE WOULD SAY HE IS IN HIS OWN HOME MINDING HIS OWN BUSINESS, AND ENJOYING THE FRUITS OF HIS LABOR. AFTER ALL, HE PAYS HIS TITHE

TO THE CHURCH AND EVERY NOW AND THEN GIVES TO THE POOR. I THINK THIS MAN COULD BE SIMILAR TO THE RICH MAN JESUS TALKED ABOUT.

PSALM 86:11-13. DAVID PRAYS FOR GOD TO TEACH HIM SO THAT HIS <u>HEART</u> WILL BE IN AGREEMENT WITH GOD. WHY? TO WALK IN TRUTH, AND BECAUSE OF GOD'S MERCY HE WAS DELIVERED FROM THE <u>LOWEST</u> HELL. A QUESTION TO PONDER IS, IF THERE IS A "LOWER" HELL IS THERE ALSO AN UPPER HELL? COULD THE RICH MAN IN LUKE BE IN THE UPPER PART SINCE HE COULD SEE ACROSS THE GULF? IF IN FACT HE WAS PUNISHED TO A LESSER DEGREE THAN OTHERS, HE WAS STILL IN HELL, IN TORMENT, DESIRING FOR JUST A TOUCH OF WATER ON HIS TONGUE. THE QUESTION FOR US IS IF OUR HEARTS WERE IN AGREEMENT WITH GOD WOULD WE NOT HAVE COMPASSION ON OTHERS, ESPECIALLY THOSE WHO ARE ON THEIR WAY TO HELL?

> ***Psalm 86:11-13*** *Teach me thy way, O LORD; I will walk in thy truth: unite my heart to fear thy name.* ***12*** *I will praise thee, O Lord my God, with all my heart: and I will glorify thy name for evermore.* ***13*** *For great is thy mercy toward me: and thou hast delivered my soul from the lowest hell.*

CHAPTER 3: HELL

LUKE 16:27-28. THE RICH MAN <u>HAD COMPASSION</u> IN HELL, BUT TOO LATE. HE SAID TO SEND LAZARUS TO WITNESS TO HIS BROTHERS. HE THOUGHT IF THEY HAD A WITNESS THEY WOULD REPENT. THE IMPLICATION HERE IS THAT <u>NO ONE</u> EVER WITNESSED TO THE RICH MAN OR HE WOULD HAVE REPENTED. NO WITNESS! SOUNDS LIKE THE WORLD WE LIVE IN DOESN'T IT? NO COMPASSION! NO WITNESS! HOW MANY PEOPLE WILL BE IN HELL BECAUSE <u>WE REALLY DON'T CARE</u>. GOD COMMANDS US TO HAVE COMPASSION AND TO WITNESS TO OTHERS. THE FIELDS ARE WHITE FOR THE HARVEST NOW! HOW MANY PEOPLE WILL GO TO HELL BECAUSE <u>WE REFUSE</u> TO HARVEST? HOW MANY?

THE QUESTION FOR EACH OF US IS, DO WE REALLY CARE? WE WON'T SATURATE OUR COUNTY WITH BIBLE TRACTS. WE WON'T TELL PEOPLE ABOUT OUR LORD AND SAVIOUR JESUS CHRIST. PEOPLE IN HELL <u>DO NOT</u> GET A SECOND CHANCE AND WE WON'T EITHER. IF IT WERE NOT FOR THE GRACE OF GOD, THE DEATH OF A FRIEND, AND A CO-WORKER WHO WOULD <u>NOT</u> GIVE UP ON ME, I COULD BE A MODERN DAY RICH MAN IN HELL.

> *Luke 16:27-28* Then he said, I pray thee therefore, father, that thou wouldest send him to my father's house: *28* For I have five brethren; that he may testify unto them, lest

they also come into this place of torment.

2 CORINTHIANS 13:5. HELL IS REAL. IT IS A PLACE OF ETERNAL TORMENT. THOSE WHO DIE WITHOUT CHRIST <u>WILL</u> GO THERE. THE LOST WILL BE JUDGED AND PUNISHED BY A JUST AND RIGHTEOUS JUDGE.

JUST LIKE REWARDS IN HEAVEN THERE ARE DEGREES OF PUNISHMENT IN HELL, BUT HELL IS <u>HELL</u>.

WHERE IS OUR HEART? DO WE REALLY CARE? DO WE REALLY LOVE JESUS?

2 Corinthians 13:5 Examine yourselves, whether ye be in the faith; prove your own selves. Know ye not your own selves, how that Jesus Christ is in you, except ye be reprobates?

FOR MANY PEOPLE THEIR OPPORTUNITY IS PAST. I AM SURE OUR GRAVEYARDS ARE FULL OF PEOPLE WHO WOULD SAY, WHY DIDN'T WE CARE! WORSE STILL WHY DIDN'T I CARE?

CHAPTER 4
HEAVEN

GENESIS 1:1. IN THE BEGINNING GOD CREATED HEAVEN. HE CREATED THREE HEAVENS, THE ATMOSPHERIC HEAVEN WHERE THE BIRDS FLY, THE CELESTIAL HEAVEN WHERE THE SUN, MOON, AND STARS ARE LOCATED, AND HEAVEN THE DWELLING PLACE OF GOD. MAN'S RELATIONSHIP TO HEAVEN IS OF GREAT INTEREST.

Genesis 1:1 In the beginning God created the heaven and the earth.

JOHN 14:1-3. MANY PEOPLE TODAY HAVE DOUBTS ABOUT A LIFE AFTER DEATH. THEY HAVE NO HOPE. OTHERS WONDER AS TO WHETHER OR NOT THERE IS AN AFTER LIFE. JESUS SAID, "LET NOT YOUR HEART BE TROUBLED" OR CONFUSED. HEAVEN IS A REAL PLACE. YOU CAN BELIEVE JESUS. HE IS GOD THE SON WHO CAN NOT LIE. JESUS TESTIFIED THAT THERE ARE MANY MANSIONS IN HEAVEN AND HE IS GOING TO PREPARE A PLACE FOR HIS PEOPLE. CAN YOU IMAGINE A PLACE DESIGNED AND BUILT BY GOD? IT WON'T BE JUST A LITTLE HOUSE ON THE HILLTOP. IT WILL BE SPECTACULAR. HE SAID HE WILL RETURN TO RECEIVE AND KEEP HIS PEOPLE WITH HIM. HE WILL RETURN TO CALL OUT ALL SAVED

PEOPLE TO BE WITH HIM FOR ALL ETERNITY. THE REAL GIFT HERE IS NOT THE MANSION OR PLACE, IT IS THE FACT THAT WE WILL FOREVER BE WITH OUR LORD AND SAVIOUR JESUS CHRIST.

> *John 14:1-3 Let not your heart be troubled: ye believe in God, believe also in me. 2 In my Father's house are many mansions: if it were not so, I would have told you. I go to prepare a place for you. 3 And if I go and prepare a place for you, I will come again, and receive you unto myself; that where I am, there ye may be also.*

2 CORINTHIANS 5:8. IF YOU ARE SAVED YOU CAN BE CONFIDENT THAT WHEN THIS EARTHLY BODY DIES YOU WILL INSTANTLY BE PRESENT WITH THE LORD. THE CARES AND TRIBULATIONS OF OUR EARTHLY LIFE WILL NO LONGER EXIST. OLD THINGS WILL HAVE PASSED AWAY AND ALL THINGS WILL BECOME NEW.

> *2 Corinthians 5:8 We are confident, I say, and willing rather to be absent from the body, and to be present with the Lord.*

PHILIPPIANS 3:20-21. GOD SAYS THAT OUR CONVERSATION IS IN HEAVEN. CONVERSATION, IN THE GREEK, MEANS CITIZENSHIP. GOD, THROUGH THE BLOOD OF JESUS CHRIST, GRANTS CITIZENSHIP IN

CHAPTER 4: HEAVEN

HEAVEN TO US. HEAVEN IS OUR COUNTRY AND OUR ETERNAL DWELLING PLACE. PRESENTLY WE ARE AMBASSADORS FOR JESUS, REPRESENTING HIM IN DECLARING THE TRUTH OF HIS HOLY WORD AND IN LEADING OTHERS TO FOLLOW HIM.

***Philippians 3:20-21** For our conversation is in heaven; from whence also we look for the Saviour, the Lord Jesus Christ: **21** Who shall change our vile body, that it may be fashioned like unto his glorious body, according to the working whereby he is able even to subdue all things unto himself.*

MATTHEW 6:19-20, 2 CORINTHIANS 5:20. A GOOD AMBASSADOR HAS A HIGHLY RESPECTED POSITION WHICH REQUIRES A LOT OF SACRIFICE AND RESPECT. IF AN AMBASSADOR FAILS TO PERFORM HE COULD BE REMOVED FROM OFFICE AND REPLACED, BUT SUCCESS IN HIS POSITION COULD ALSO LEAD TO AN AMBASSADORSHIP IN A MORE IMPORTANT COUNTRY. AS CHRISTIANS WE START AT THE TOP BY REPRESENTING HEAVEN. JESUS IMPLORES US TO BE <u>HIS</u> AMBASSADORS IN <u>HIS</u> PLACE. ARE WE? WE COULD RECEIVE NO HIGHER HONOR. IF SUCCESSFUL, INCORRUPTIBLE TREASURES IN HEAVEN WILL BE OUR WAGES. WE SHOULD NOT GROW COMPLACENT AND NEGLECT SO GREAT A RESPONSIBILITY.

JESUS SAID THAT IF YOU LOVE HIM YOU WILL KEEP HIS COMMANDMENTS.

Matthew 6:19-20. *Lay not up for yourselves treasures upon earth, where moth and rust doth corrupt, and where thieves break through and steal:* ***20*** *But lay up for yourselves treasures in heaven, where neither moth nor rust doth corrupt, and where thieves do not break through nor steal:*

2 Corinthians 5:20. *Now then we are ambassadors for Christ, as though God did beseech you by us: we pray you in Christ's stead, be ye reconciled to God.*

ISAIAH 64:4; 1 CORINTHIANS 2:9. HAVE YOU EVER IMAGINED YOURSELF RECEIVING SOME GREAT GIFT THAT WOULD BE IMPOSSIBLE FOR YOU TO OBTAIN? MOST OF US HAVE. GOD SAID YOU CAN'T EVEN IMAGINE THE THINGS (PLURAL) THAT HE HAS PREPARED FOR THOSE WHO LOVE HIM. I CAN IMAGINE A LOT OF THINGS SUCH AS A FISHING BOAT, A NEW TRUCK, A MANSION, OR EVEN A GREAT POSITION; BUT THESE THINGS ARE NOT EVEN IN THE BALLPARK WITH RESPECT TO WHAT GOD HAS PREPARED.

Isaiah 64:4 *For since the beginning of the world men have not heard, nor perceived by the ear,*

CHAPTER 4: HEAVEN

neither hath the eye seen, O God, beside thee, what he hath prepared for him that waiteth for him.

1 Corinthians 2:9 *But as it is written, Eye hath not seen, nor ear heard, neither have entered into the heart of man, the things which God hath prepared for them that love him.*

ISAIAH 14:13-14. LUCIFER (SATAN) REBELLED AGAINST GOD SAYING HE WOULD ASCEND INTO HEAVEN IN THE SIDES OF THE NORTH. THIS INDICATES THAT HEAVEN, GOD'S DWELLING PLACE, IS CURRENTLY IN THE THIRD HEAVEN BEYOND THE CELESTIAL HEAVEN IN THE NORTH.

Isaiah 14:13-14 *For thou hast said in thine heart, I will ascend into heaven, I will exalt my throne above the stars of God: I will sit also upon the mount of the congregation, in the sides of the north:* ***14*** *I will ascend above the heights of the clouds; I will be like the most High.*

REVELATION 21:1-3. JOHN SAW A NEW HEAVEN AND A NEW EARTH, THE FINAL ABODE OF GOD. HEAVEN WILL BE ON EARTH. THIS NEW EARTH WILL NO LONGER CONTAIN SIN. IT WILL BE PURIFIED BY FIRE AND MADE NEW. IT WILL CONTAIN MUCH MORE LAND MASS SINCE THERE WILL BE NO MORE SEA. JOHN SAW A NEW JERUSALEM PREPARED AS A BRIDE ADORNED FOR HER

HUSBAND. THE SPLENDER OF THIS CITY IS UNIMAGINABLE TO OUR MINDS. GOD DEMONSTRATED HIS PRESENCE IN THE TABERNACLE IN THE WILDERNESS BY A CLOUD BY DAY AND FIRE BY NIGHT. GOD WILL BE THE LIGHT OF THIS NEW WORLD. IN THIS NEW EARTH GOD'S TABERNACLE WILL BE <u>WITH</u> HIS PEOPLE AND HE WILL BE THEIR GOD. DEATH, SORROW, CRYING, AND PAIN WILL NO LONGER EXIST. GOD AND MAN WILL DWELL TOGETHER IN A PERFECT ENVIRONMENT.

*Revelation 21:1-3 And I saw a new heaven and a new earth: for the first heaven and the first earth were passed away; and there was no more sea. **2** And I John saw the holy city, new Jerusalem, coming down from God out of heaven, prepared as a bride adorned for her husband. **3** And I heard a great voice out of heaven saying, Behold, the tabernacle of God is with men, and he will dwell with them, and they shall be his people, and God himself shall be with them, and be their God.*

REVELATION 21:7. SAVED PEOPLE WILL BE JOINT HEIRS WITH JESUS CHRIST AND WILL INHERIT ALL THINGS. WE WILL BE SONS (AND DAUGHTERS) OF GOD AND HE WILL BE OUR GOD. (STOP! THINK HOW WONDERFUL THIS WILL BE. WE WILL HAVE

CHAPTER 4: HEAVEN

A DIVINE PLACE IN THE PRESENCE OF GOD. COULD ANYTHING EVER BE BETTER?)

Revelation 21:7 He that overcometh shall inherit all things; and I will be his God, and he shall be my son.

REVELATION 21:16. THE CITY OF NEW JERUSALEM WILL BE A CUBE. THE LENGTH, BREADTH, AND HEIGHT WILL MEASURE 1,500 MILES EACH.

Revelation 21:16 And the city lieth foursquare, and the length is as large as the breadth: and he measured the city with the reed, twelve thousand furlongs. The length and the breadth and the height of it are equal.

REVELATION 21:22-27. THERE WILL BE NO TEMPLE IN THE NEW JERUSALEM. THE LORD GOD ALMIGHTY AND THE LAMB WILL BE THE TEMPLE. NO LONGER WILL WE NEED A HIGH PRIEST TO INTERCEDE BETWEEN US AND GOD. WE WILL HAVE COMPLETE FREEDOM AND DIRECT ACCESS TO OUR GOD. THERE WILL BE NO NEED FOR THE SUN OR ANY ARTIFICIAL LIGHT FOR THE SHEKINAH GLORY OF GOD AND THE LAMB (JESUS) WILL BE ALL SUFFICIENT TO PERFECTLY PROVIDE LIGHT FOR EVERY NEED. THE NEW JERUSALEM WILL BE THE CENTER OF EVERYTHING WORLDWIDE. EVERYONE, INCLUDING THE KINGS OF THE EARTH, WILL

ARE YOU READY?

COME TO NEW JERUSALEM TO WORSHIP, HONOR, AND BRING THEIR GLORY TO WALK IN THE <u>LIGHT</u> OF GOD THE FATHER AND GOD THE SON. THE GATES OF THE CITY WILL ALWAYS BE OPEN BECAUSE THE <u>LIGHT</u> NEVER DIMS NOR CEASES. IT WILL ALWAYS BE DAY. ONLY THOSE WHOSE NAMES ARE WRITTEN IN THE LAMB'S BOOK OF LIFE WILL EVER ENTER THE NEW JERUSALEM.

***Revelation 21:22-27** And I saw no temple therein: for the Lord God Almighty and the Lamb are the temple of it. **23** And the city had no need of the sun, neither of the moon, to shine in it: for the glory of God did lighten it, and the Lamb is the light thereof. **24** And the nations of them which are saved shall walk in the light of it: and the kings of the earth do bring their glory and honour into it. **25** And the gates of it shall not be shut at all by day: for there shall be no night there. **26** And they shall bring the glory and honour of the nations into it. **27** And there shall in no wise enter into it any thing that defileth, neither whatsoever worketh abomination, or maketh a lie: but they which are written in the Lamb's book of life.*

REVELATION 22:1-4. I USED TO SWIM IN WAKULLA SPRINGS NEAR TALLAHASSEE, FLORIDA. IF I REMEMBER CORRECTLY IT IS

CHAPTER 4: HEAVEN

THE LARGEST SPRING IN THE UNITED STATES, AND MAYBE THE WORLD. IT IS VERY DEEP AND <u>WAS</u> CRYSTAL CLEAR. ONE DIVING FROM THE TOWER HAD TO HAVE SOMEONE RIPPLE THE SURFACE TO IDENTIFY THE WATER, OTHERWISE YOU WOUD ONLY SEE THE BOTTOM AND WOULD LIKELY DO A BELLY BUST. CAN YOU IMAGINE THE PURITY OF THE WATER WHEN IT IS PURIFIED BY GOD? CAN YOU IMAGINE THE RIVER FLOWING FROM THE ACTUAL THRONE OF GOD AND JESUS? CAN YOU IMAGINE THE TREE OF LIFE PROBABLY IN ROWS ON EITHER SIDE OF THE RIVER OF LIFE HAVING A DIFFERENT FRUIT EACH MONTH, AND LEAVES FOR HEALING THE NATIONS? NO WORMS, NO DROUGHT, OR ANYTHING WOULD CONTAMINATE THE WATER, FRUIT, OR THE LEAVES. THE BEAUTY OF THE EARTH, WITH ALL THE ANIMALS AND BIRDS WILL BE A SIGHT TO BEHOLD. CAN YOU IMAGINE BEING ABLE TO LOOK UPON THE FACE OF JESUS CHRIST WHO PAID SUCH A HIGH PRICE TO REDEEM OUR SOULS? CAN YOU IMAGINE BEING ABLE TO SERVE HIM IN SUCH AN ENVIRONMENT FOR ALL ETERNITY? CAN YOU IMAGINE? NOW IMAGINE THAT WE <u>CAN'T</u> IMAGINE WHAT GOD HATH PREPARED FOR US.

***Revelation 22:1-4** And he shewed me a pure river of water of life, clear as crystal, proceeding out of the throne of God and of the Lamb. **2** In the midst of the street of it, and on* *either side of the river, was there the tree of life, which bare twelve manner of fruits, and yielded her fruit every month: and the leaves of the tree were for the healing of the nations. **3** And there shall be no more curse: but the throne of God and of the Lamb shall be in it; and his servants shall serve him: **4** And they shall see his face; and his name shall be in their foreheads.*

MARK 13:31-37. GOD'S WORDS ARE FOREVER SETTLED IN HEAVEN. THEY ARE TRUE AND SHOULD GOVERN EVERY LIFE. WE ARE GIVEN A STERN WARNING TO PREPARE FOR THE RETURN OF JESUS. WHEN HE COMES FOR HIS CHURCH (SAVED PEOPLE), IT WILL BE TOO LATE FOR THOSE LEFT BEHIND. THEY WILL BE GIVEN A STRONG DELUSION. WILL HE FIND YOU SLEEPING? JESUS SAID, "I SAY UNTO ALL, WATCH."

***Mark 13:31-37** Heaven and earth shall pass away: but my words shall not pass away. **32** But of that day and that hour knoweth no man, no, not the angels which are in heaven, neither the Son, but the Father. **33** Take ye heed, watch and pray: for ye know not when the time is. **34** For the Son of man is as a man taking a far journey, who left his house, and gave authority to his servants, and to every man his work,*

CHAPTER 4: HEAVEN

and commanded the porter to watch. **35** *Watch ye therefore: for ye know not when the master of the house cometh, at even, or at midnight, or at the cockcrowing, or in the morning:* **36** *Lest coming suddenly he find you sleeping.* **37** *And what I say unto you I say unto all, Watch.*

GET READY! JESUS IS COMING SOON. WATCH!

CHAPTER 5
JESUS CHRIST

IS JESUS CHRIST REAL? THIS IS QUESTIONED MORE AND MORE IN THIS SO-CALLED MODERN AGE. WE LIVE IN A WONDERFUL LAND OF OPPORTUNITY IN AMERICA, BUT WE ARE ON A VERY SLIPPERY SLOPE IN TURNING AWAY FROM KNOWING JESUS AS OUR LORD AND SAVIOUR.

A CURSORY REVIEW OF GOD'S HOLY WORD (THE KING JAMES BIBLE) WILL PROVE BEYOND ANY DOUBT THAT JESUS IS THE CHRIST, GOD THE SON, WHO CAME TO THIS EARTH FOR ONE PURPOSE AND THAT IS TO SAVE SINNERS. THERE ARE LITERALLY HUNDREDS OF PROPHESIES IN THE BIBLE CONCERNING JESUS. TODAY WE CAN LOOK BACK ON HISTORY AND SEE MANY THAT HAVE COME TO PASS EXACTLY AS PROPHESIED. THIS OFFERS PROOF THAT THOSE REMAINING WILL ALSO BE FULFILLED. THE FIRST REFERENCE TO JESUS (GENESIS 3:15) REVEALS THAT HE WILL BE OF THE SEED OF EVE WHO WILL BRUISE THE HEAD OF SATAN. THE LAST REFERENCE IS THE LAST VERSE IN THE BIBLE (REVELATION 22:21) WHERE JESUS HAS GAINED TOTAL VICTORY AND BESTOWS HIS BLESSINGS ON EVERYONE.

KNOWING JESUS AS TO WHO HE IS AND WHAT HE IS, AND ACCEPTING BY FAITH

THE FACT THAT HE DID DIE FOR YOUR SINS WILL PUT YOU ON A SOLID PATH TO SALVATION.

TO WHET YOUR APPETITE, FOLLOWING WILL BE A FEW OF THESE PROPHESIES AND THEIR FULFILLMENTS.

DANIEL 9:24-25. THE EXACT TIME OF JESUS' 2ND COMING IS REVEALED. "WEEKS" HERE IS A UNIT OF MEASUREMENT LIKE A POUND, BUT A POUND OF WHAT? "WEEKS" HERE MEANS SEVEN, BUT SEVEN WHAT? A CAREFUL STUDY REVEALS IT TO BE SEVEN YEARS. THEREFORE, SEVENTY WEEKS CAN BE SHOWN TO BE SEVEN TIMES SEVENTY OR FOUR HUNDRED AND NINETY YEARS. THIS REVEALS THE EXACT TIME THE MESSIAH WILL BE "CUT OFF."

> ***Daniel 9:24-25** Seventy weeks are determined upon thy people and upon thy holy city, to finish the transgression, and to make an end of sins, and to make reconciliation for iniquity, and to bring in everlasting righteousness, and to seal up the vision and prophecy, and to anoint the most Holy. **25** Know therefore and understand, that from the going forth of the commandment to restore and to build Jerusalem unto the Messiah the Prince shall be seven weeks, and threescore and two weeks: the street shall be built again, and the wall, even in troublous times.*

CHAPTER 5: JESUS CHRIST

ISAIAH 7:14; MATTHEW 1:18-23. JESUS WAS BORN OF A VIRGIN. HAD JESUS BEEN BORN OF A MAN AND WOMAN HE WOULD HAVE BEEN A SINNER AND COULD NOT HAVE SAVED HIMSELF, LET ALONE YOU AND ME. HE WAS GOD, THE SON, WHO PUT ON THE FLESH OF MAN AND BECAME 100% MAN, ALL THE WHILE MAINTAINING HIS SOVEREIGNTY AS 100% GOD. THE NAME IMMANUEL MEANS "GOD WITH US." THE ANGEL OF THE LORD CONFIRMED TO JOSEPH THAT MARY'S CHILD WAS OF THE HOLY GHOST (NOT MAN), AND HE WOULD BE NAMED JESUS. HIS PURPOSE WAS TO SAVE HIS PEOPLE FROM THEIR SINS.

***Isaiah 7:14** Therefore the Lord himself shall give you a sign; Behold, a virgin shall conceive, and bear a son, and shall call his name Immanuel.*

***Matthew 1:18-23** Now the birth of Jesus Christ was on this wise: When as his mother Mary was espoused to Joseph, before they came together, she was found with child of the Holy Ghost. **19** Then Joseph her husband, being a just man, and not willing to make her a publick example, was minded to put her away privily. **20** But while he thought on these things, behold, the angel of the Lord appeared unto him in a dream, saying, Joseph, thou son of David,* *fear not to take unto thee Mary thy wife: for that which is conceived in her is of the Holy Ghost.* **21** *And she shall bring forth a son, and thou shalt call his name JESUS: for he shall save his people from their sins.* **22** *Now all this was done, that it might be fulfilled which was spoken of the Lord by the prophet, saying,* **23** *Behold, a virgin shall be with child, and shall bring forth a son, and they shall call his name Emmanuel, which being interpreted is, God with us.*

MICAH 5:2; MATTHEW 2:1, 5:6. THE PLACE OF THE BIRTH OF JESUS WAS TO BE BETHLEHEM EPHRATAH; A SPECIFIC TOWN NAMED BETHLEHEM BUT LOCATED IN JUDAH A FEW MILES SOUTHWEST OF JERUSALEM. THE WISE MEN WHO SEARCHING FOR JESUS KNEW EXACTLY WHO JESUS WAS AND WHERE HE WOULD BE BORN BY THEIR EXTENSIVE KNOWLEDGE OF OLD TESTAMENT PROPHECY.

***Micah 5:2** But thou, Bethlehem Ephratah, though thou be little among the thousands of Judah, yet out of thee shall he come forth unto me that is to be ruler in Israel; whose goings forth have been from of old, from everlasting.*

***Matthew 2:1** Now when Jesus was born in Bethlehem of Judaea in the days of Herod the king, behold,*

CHAPTER 5: JESUS CHRIST

there came wise men from the east to Jerusalem,

Matthew 5:6 *Blessed are they which do hunger and thirst after righteousness: for they shall be filled.*

PSALM 2:1-3; ACTS 4:25-27. JESUS PROVED HIMSELF TO BE THE SON OF GOD IN MANY WAYS, BUT MOST NOTABLY BY THE MANY MIRACLES THAT HE PERFORMED, INCLUDING HEALING THE SICK, FEEDING THE MULTITUDE, AND RAISING THE DEAD. YET HE WAS REJECTED BY THE RULERS, THE GENTILES, AND THE PEOPLE OF ISRAEL. PROPHECY FORETOLD OF HIS REJECTION AND HISTORY PROVED IT TO BE CORRECT.

Psalm 2:1-3 *Why do the heathen rage, and the people imagine a vain thing?* **2** *The kings of the earth set themselves, and the rulers take counsel together, against the LORD, and against his anointed, saying,* **3** *Let us break their bands asunder, and cast away their cords from us.*

Acts 4:25-27 *Who by the mouth of thy servant David hast said, Why did the heathen rage, and the people imagine vain things?* **26** *The kings of the earth stood up, and the rulers were gathered together against the Lord, and against his Christ.* **27** *For of a truth against thy holy child Jesus, whom thou hast anointed, both*

Herod, and Pontius Pilate, with the Gentiles, and the people of Israel, were gathered together,

ZECHARIAH 9:9; MATTHEW 21:1-9. PROPHECY FORETOLD THAT JESUS WOULD TRIUMPHANTLY ENTER JERUSALEM RIDING ON A DONKEY. WHEN HE ENTERED JERUSALEM THE PEOPLE ACCEPTED HIM AS THE LONG-AWAITED MESSIAH, BUT COULD IT HAVE BEEN BECAUSE THEY WANTED A KING WHO WOULD MULTIPLY THEIR FOOD SUPPLY AS HE DID WITH THE FIVE LOAVES AND TWO FISH? WHAT A MARVELOUS ENTRY AND GLORIOUS EVENT THIS MUST HAVE BEEN WITH THE PEOPLE SAYING "HOSANNA TO THE SON OF DAVID. BLESSED IS HE THAT COMETH IN THE NAME OF THE LORD. HOSANNA TO THE HIGHEST." HOSANNA IN THE GREEK MEANS "SAVE NOW" OR "SAVE WE PRAY THEE." THIS PRAISE WAS SHORT-LIVED FOR AS THE DAY ENDS HE WOULD BE REJECTED.

***Zechariah 9:9** Rejoice greatly, O daughter of Zion; shout, O daughter of Jerusalem: behold, thy King cometh unto thee: he is just, and having salvation; lowly, and riding upon an ass, and upon a colt the foal of an ass.*

***Matthew 21:1-9** And when they drew nigh unto Jerusalem, and were come to Bethphage, unto the mount of Olives, then sent Jesus two*

CHAPTER 5: JESUS CHRIST

*disciples, **2** Saying unto them, Go into the village over against you, and straightway ye shall find an ass tied, and a colt with her: loose them, and bring them unto me. **3** And if any man say ought unto you, ye shall say, The Lord hath need of them; and straightway he will send them. **4** All this was done, that it might be fulfilled which was spoken by the prophet, saying, **5** Tell ye the daughter of Sion, Behold, thy King cometh unto thee, meek, and sitting upon an ass, and a colt the foal of an ass. **6** And the disciples went, and did as Jesus commanded them, **7** And brought the ass, and the colt, and put on them their clothes, and they set him thereon. **8** And a very great multitude spread their garments in the way; others cut down branches from the trees, and strawed them in the way. **9** And the multitudes that went before, and that followed, cried, saying, Hosanna to the Son of David: Blessed is he that cometh in the name of the Lord; Hosanna in the highest.*

PSALM 41:9, MATTHEW 26:24-25. JUDAS WAS A DISCIPLE OF JESUS WHO ATE WITH HIM, SLEPT WITH HIM, AND LIVED WITH HIM. HE WAS PRESENT WHILE JESUS PERFORMED MANY MIRACLES. HE WAS A FAMILIAR FRIEND AND WAS TRUSTED BY JESUS. HE SERVED AS THE KEEPER OF THE

BAG OR TREASURER. HE HAD A HEAD KNOWLEDGE OF WHO JESUS WAS, BUT HE DID NOT HAVE A HEART KNOWLEDGE. JUDAS CALLED JESUS MASTER, NOT MESSIAH. HE BETRAYED JESUS WHO CALLED HIM FRIEND. JESUS SAID IT WOULD HAVE BEEN BETTER FOR JUDAS IF HE HAD NEVER BEEN BORN.

***Psalm 41:9** Yea, mine own familiar friend, in whom I trusted, which did eat of my bread, hath lifted up his heel against me.*

***Matthew 26:24-25** The Son of man goeth as it is written of him: but woe unto that man by whom the Son of man is betrayed! it had been good for that man if he had not been born. **25** Then Judas, which betrayed him, answered and said, Master, is it I? He said unto him, Thou hast said.*

ZECHARIAH 11:12; MATTHEW 26:14-16. JESUS HAD GREAT LOVE FOR HIS PEOPLE. RECOGNIZING THE PEOPLE'S PRIDE AND LACK OF ACCEPTANCE AS TO WHO HE WAS AND WHAT HE HAD DONE FOR THEM HE SAID "GIVE ME MY PRICE OR FORBEAR." THEY PAID HIM THIRTY PIECES OF SILVER, THE PRICE OF A BOND SERVANT. WHAT JESUS WANTED WAS THEIR LOVE AND FOR THEM TO SEE HIM FOR WHO HE WAS, THEIR MESSIAH. JUDAS FULFILLED THIS PROPHECY BY CONTRACTING WITH THE PRIEST FOR THIRTY PIECES OF SILVER TO

CHAPTER 5: JESUS CHRIST

BETRAY JESUS. THIS AMOUNTED TO ABOUT A MONTH'S WAGES OR THE PRICE OF A COMMON SLAVE. THE SAME GREEK WORD "BETRAY" IN VERSE 16 IS TRANSLATED "DELIVER" IN VERSE 15. JUDAS FOLLOWED THROUGH WITH HIS END OF THE BARGAIN BY IDENTIFYING JESUS TO HIS ENEMIES WITH A KISS IN THE GARDEN OF GETHSEMANE. JUDAS HAD REMORSE (NOT FAITH) AND HANGED HIMSELF.

Zechariah 11:12 And I said unto them, If ye think good, give me my price; and if not, forbear. So they weighed for my price thirty pieces of silver.

Matthew 26:14-16 Then one of the twelve, called Judas Iscariot, went unto the chief priests, 15 And said unto them, What will ye give me, and I will deliver him unto you? And they covenanted with him for thirty pieces of silver. 16 And from that time he sought opportunity to betray him.

THERE ARE MANY PROPHESIES CONCERNING THE TIME FROM THE ARREST OF JESUS TO HIS ASCENSION INTO HEAVEN. A FEW OF THESE ARE AS FOLLOWS:

ISAIAH 53:4-6; 1 PETER 3:18. VERSE 4 BEGINS WITH THE WORD "SURELY" WHICH DIRECTS OUR ATTENTION TO THE TRUTH THAT FOLLOWS. THE "HE" COULD BE NO

ARE YOU READY?

OTHER THAN THE MESSIAH, OUR LORD AND SAVIOUR JESUS CHRIST. HE BORE OUR GRIEFS AND OUR SORROWS. HE WAS WOUNDED, BRUISED, AND WHIPPED FOR OUR INIQUITY AND OUR TRANSGRESSIONS. CHRIST DID IN FACT, SOME 300 YEARS LATER, SUFFER FOR OUR SINS, THE JUST FOR THE UNJUST, FOR ONE PURPOSE; TO OPEN UP THE ONE WAY WHICH COULD LEAD US TO GOD. WHAT A SAVIOUR!!

Isaiah 53:4-6 Surely he hath borne our griefs, and carried our sorrows: yet we did esteem him stricken, smitten of God, and afflicted. 5 But he was wounded for our transgressions, he was bruised for our iniquities: the chastisement of our peace was upon him; and with his stripes we are healed. 6 All we like sheep have gone astray; we have turned every one to his own way; and the LORD hath laid on him the iniquity of us all.

1 Peter 3:18 For Christ also hath once suffered for sins, the just for the unjust, that he might bring us to God, being put to death in the flesh, but quickened by the Spirit:

ZECHARIAH 12:10; JOHN 20:27-28. THE JEWISH NATION WILL FINALLY SEE JESUS AS THEIR MESSIAH WITH THE OUTPOURING OF THE HOLY SPIRIT. THEY WILL SEE THE ONE WHOM THEY PIERCED AFTER DENYING

CHAPTER 5: JESUS CHRIST

HIM FOR HUNDREDS OF YEARS. THEY WILL RECOGNIZE THE PIERCING OF HIS SIDE AS THE FINAL ACT OF ALL THE PUNISHMENT WHICH HE HAD TO SUFFER TO SAVE THEIR SOULS. THEY WILL MOURN AND BE IN BITTERNESS FOR JESUS AS THEY WOULD HAD THEY LOST THEIR ONLY SON.

AFTER JESUS HAD BEEN CRUCIFIED, BURIED, RISEN FROM THE TOMB, AND SEEN BY MANY, THE DISCIPLE THOMAS SAID: "EXCEPT I SHALL SEE IN HIS HANDS THE PRINT OF THE NAILS, AND PUT MY FINGER INTO THE PRINT OF THE NAILS, AND THRUST MY HAND INTO HIS SIDE, I WILL NOT BELIEVE." THIS IS WHERE WE GET THE PHRASE, "DOUBTING THOMAS." EIGHT DAYS LATER JESUS GAVE THOMAS THIS OPPORTUNITY HE NEEDED. CAN YOU IMAGINE THE SHAME THOMAS FELT WHEN HEARING THE WORDS OF JESUS? FOR THOSE WHO DO NOT SEE JESUS IN THEIR LIFETIME, THIS FEELING WILL BE COMPOUNDED AT THE GREAT WHITE THRONE JUDGMENT SEAT OF CHRIST.

> ***Zechariah 12:10*** *And I will pour upon the house of David, and upon the inhabitants of Jerusalem, the spirit of grace and of supplications: and they shall look upon me whom they have pierced, and they shall mourn for him, as one mourneth for his only son, and shall be in bitterness*

for him, as one that is in bitterness for his firstborn.

John 20:27-28 *Then saith he to Thomas, Reach hither thy finger, and behold my hands; and reach hither thy hand, and thrust it into my side: and be not faithless, but believing.* ***28*** *And Thomas answered and said unto him, My Lord and my God.*

PSALM 22:6-8; MATTHEW 27: 26-31. PROPHECY PREDICTED THAT JESUS WOULD FEEL LIKE A WORM WHILE HANGING ON THE CROSS. AFTER ALL THE GOOD HE DID AND THE MIRACLES THAT HE ACCOMPLISHED BEFORE THE PEOPLE, THEY REJECTED HIM AND DEMANDED THAT HE BE CRUCIFIED. HE WAS INNOCENT. YET HAVING COMMITTED NO WRONG THEY WOULD TURN ON HIM AS IF HE WERE SOME VILE, EVIL PERSON. THEY WOULD LAUGH, SHAKE THEIR HEADS, AND PUCKER UP THEIR LIPS IN RIDICULE AND HATE. JESUS WOULD BE INSULTED, MOCKED, AND REJECTED.

YEARS LATER THE PEOPLE DID TURN ON JESUS JUST LIKE PROPHECY FORETOLD. EVEN THOUGH PILATE THOUGHT HIM INNOCENT, HE STILL HAD HIM SCOURGED AND TURNED HIM OVER TO THE PRIESTS AND HIS FOLLOWERS TO BE CRUCIFIED. SCOURGING WAS PERFORMED WITH A LEATHER WHIP CONSISTING OF SEVERAL THONGS WHOSE ENDS WERE EMBEDDED

CHAPTER 5: JESUS CHRIST

WITH SHARP BONE OR METAL. THEY WOULD LASH HIM FORTY TIMES SAVE ONE. THE LAW FORBADE LASHING OVER FORTY TIMES OR ELSE THE LASHER WOULD BE IN SERIOUS TROUBLE. THE "SAVE ONE" WAS JUST TO BE ON THE SAFE SIDE. MANY DIED BECAUSE SCOURGING WOULD OPEN UP THEIR INSIDES OR THEY WOULD BLEED TO DEATH. AS IF THAT WERE NOT ENOUGH, THEY ADDED MORE TORTURE AND SHAME TO THEIR EVIL. THEY STRIPPED HIM OF HIS CLOTHES AND MOCKED HIM WITH A ROBE AND A CROWN OF THORNS SAYING "HAIL, KING OF THE JEWS!" THEY THEN STRUCK HIS CROWNED HEAD WITH A REED BEFORE NAILING HIM TO A CROSS. THE TORTURE, HUMILIATION, AND MOCKERY ARE BEYOND OUR ABILITY TO UNDERSTAND. SINCE HE WAS AND IS THE SON OF GOD HE COULD HAVE CALLED A LEGION OF ANGELS TO SET HIM FREE BUT CHOSE TO PAY FOR OUR REDEMPTION WITH HIS PRECIOUS BLOOD. HALLELUJAH, WHAT A SAVIOUR!

> ***Psalm 22:6-8** But I am a worm, and no man; a reproach of men, and despised of the people. **7** All they that see me laugh me to scorn: they shoot out the lip, they shake the head, saying, **8** He trusted on the LORD that he would deliver him: let him deliver him, seeing he delighted in him.*

***Matthew 27:26-31** Then released he Barabbas unto them: and when he had scourged Jesus, he delivered him to be crucified. **27** Then the soldiers of the governor took Jesus into the common hall, and gathered unto him the whole band of soldiers. **28** And they stripped him, and put on him a scarlet robe. **29** And when they had platted a crown of thorns, they put it upon his head, and a reed in his right hand: and they bowed the knee before him, and mocked him, saying, Hail, King of the Jews! **30** And they spit upon him, and took the reed, and smote him on the head. **31** And after that they had mocked him, they took the robe off from him, and put his own raiment on him, and led him away to crucify him.*

ISAIAH 53:9; MATTHEW 27:38, 57-60. PROPHECY SAID JESUS MADE HIS GRAVE WITH THE WICKED AND WITH THE RICH IN HIS DEATH. THESE TWO PROPHESIES WERE FULFILLED WHEN JESUS DIED ON THE CROSS CLOSE TO 2,800 YEARS LATER. THE BIBLE (HISTORY) RECORDS THAT HE WAS CRUCIFIED BETWEEN TWO THIEVES, WHO WERE WICKED MEN, BEING PUNISHED FOR THEIR SINS. (IT IS IMPORTANT TO NOTE THAT ONE OF THESE THIEVES REPENTED OF HIS SINS, TRUSTED JESUS, AND WAS SAVED. THIS CONFIRMS THE FACT THAT NO MATTER HOW EVIL ONE MAY BE, THEY <u>CAN</u>

CHAPTER 5: JESUS CHRIST

BE SAVED. JESUS DIED FOR SINNERS; <u>ALL</u> SINNERS.

Isaiah 53:9 And he made his grave with the wicked, and with the rich in his death; because he had done no violence, neither was any deceit in his mouth.

Matthew 27:38 Then were there two thieves crucified with him, one on the right hand, and another on the left.

Matthew 27:57-60 When the even was come, there came a rich man of Arimathaea, named Joseph, who also himself was Jesus' disciple: 58 He went to Pilate, and begged the body of Jesus. Then Pilate commanded the body to be delivered. 59 And when Joseph had taken the body, he wrapped it in a clean linen cloth, 60 And laid it in his own new tomb, which he had hewn out in the rock: and he rolled a great stone to the door of the sepulchre, and departed.

JOHN 19:38-42. JOSEPH WAS A RICH MAN AND A SECRET DISCIPLE OF JESUS. WHEN JESUS WAS CRUCIFIED HE OPENLY DECLARED HIS FAITH AT THE RISK OF HIS OWN LIFE BY ASKING PILATE FOR JESUS' BODY. HE AND NICODEMUS PREPARED

JESUS' BODY AND PLACED IT IN JOSEPH'S OWN NEW TOMB.

John 19:38-42 And after this Joseph of Arimathaea, being a disciple of Jesus, but secretly for fear of the Jews, besought Pilate that he might take away the body of Jesus: and Pilate gave him leave. He came therefore, and took the body of Jesus. 39 And there came also Nicodemus, which at the first came to Jesus by night, and brought a mixture of myrrh and aloes, about an hundred pound weight. 40 Then took they the body of Jesus, and wound it in linen clothes with the spices, as the manner of the Jews is to bury. 41 Now in the place where he was crucified there was a garden; and in the garden a new sepulchre, wherein was never man yet laid. 42 There laid they Jesus therefore because of the Jews' preparation day; for the sepulchre was nigh at hand.

PSALM 68:18; EPHESIANS 4:8. IF JESUS HAD STAYED IN THE TOMB THERE WOULD BE NO HOPE OF OUR OWN RESURRECTION, BUT HE DIDN'T. HE ASCENDED INTO HEAVEN AND NOW SITS ON THE RIGHT HAND OF GOD AS OUR ADVOCATE. (HE NEVER LOSES A CASE.) THE SOULS OF THE RIGHTEOUS DEAD WERE IN THE PARADISE SECTION IN THE EARTH

CHAPTER 5: JESUS CHRIST

BEFORE THE CROSS (LUKE 16: 19-31). DURING THE THREE DAYS BEFORE HIS RESURRECTION HE DESCENDED INTO PARADISE AND MOVED IT WITH THE RIGHTEOUS DEAD INTO HEAVEN WHERE THEY NOW RESIDE. JESUS BY HIS CRUCIFICTION, DEATH, RESURRECTION, AND ASCENSION INTO HEAVEN CONQUERED DEATH, HELL, AND THE GRAVE. "GAVE GIFTS" DESCRIBES THE ACTS OF A CONQUERER WHO HAVING RECEIVED THE SPOILS DISTRIBUTES THEM TO HIS FRIENDS. JESUS GAVE AND WE RECEIVED THE GIFT OF SALVATION BY BELIEVING IN HIM. THE LORD IS COMING AGAIN TO SET UP HIS KINGDOM AND WILL DWELL AMONG ALL THOSE WHO ARE SAVED.

Psalm 68:18 Thou hast ascended on high, thou hast led captivity captive: thou hast received gifts for men; yea, for the rebellious also, that the LORD God might dwell among them.

Ephesians 4:8 Wherefore he saith, When he ascended up on high, he led captivity captive, and gave gifts unto men.

LUKE 24:1-8, 50-51, 1 CORINTHIANS 15:6. ON THE FIRST DAY OF THE WEEK AFTER THREE DAYS AND THREE NIGHTS, THE TOMB OF JESUS WAS FOUND TO BE EMPTY. TWO ANGELS TESTIFIED THAT HE HAD RISEN. AFTER THAT HE WAS SEEN BY HIS

ARE YOU READY?

DISCIPLES, OTHERS, AND ABOVE FIVE HUNDRED AT THE SAME TIME BEFORE HIS ASCENSION INTO HEAVEN.

Luke 24:1-8 Now upon the first day of the week, very early in the morning, they came unto the sepulchre, bringing the spices which they had prepared, and certain others with them. **2** And they found the stone rolled away from the sepulchre. **3** And they entered in, and found not the body of the Lord Jesus. **4** And it came to pass, as they were much perplexed thereabout, behold, two men stood by them in shining garments: **5** And as they were afraid, and bowed down their faces to the earth, they said unto them, Why seek ye the living among the dead? **6** He is not here, but is risen: remember how he spake unto you when he was yet in Galilee, **7** Saying, The Son of man must be delivered into the hands of sinful men, and be crucified, and the third day rise again. **8** And they remembered his words,

Luke 24:50-51 And he led them out as far as to Bethany, and he lifted up his hands, and blessed them. **51** And it came to pass, while he blessed them, he was parted from them, and carried up into heaven.

CHAPTER 5: JESUS CHRIST

*1 **Corinthians 15:6** After that, he was seen of above five hundred brethren at once; of whom the greater part remain unto this present, but some are fallen asleep.*

GALATIANS 4:4-7. FULNESS OF TIME IS THE TIME DETERMINED BY GOD. "GOD SENT FORTH HIS SON" TO REDEEM MAN THAT WE MIGHT RECEIVE THE ADOPTION OF SONS. HE ALSO SENT THE HOLY SPIRIT INTO OUR HEARTS. BY HIS FREE GIFT, AND OUR TRUST IN HIM WE BECOME SONS OF GOD AND JOINT HEIRS OF CHRIST. HE IS OUR LOVING FATHER WHO CARES FOR US AS FAMILY MEMBERS. WHAT LOVE!

***Galatians 4:4-7** But when the fulness of the time was come, God sent forth his Son, made of a woman, made under the law, **5** To redeem them that were under the law, that we might receive the adoption of sons. **6** And because ye are sons, God hath sent forth the Spirit of his Son into your hearts, crying, Abba, Father. **7** Wherefore thou art no more a servant, but a son; and if a son, then an heir of God through Christ.*

ACTS 1:3, 9-11. JESUS WAS SEEN FORTY DAYS <u>AFTER</u> HIS RESURRECTION FROM THE TOMB. BY MANY INFALLIBLE TRUTHS THESE FACTS CANNOT BE DENIED. HE WAS SEEN ASCENDING INTO HEAVEN

ARE YOU READY?

AND TWO ANGELS TESTIFIED THAT HE WILL COME AGAIN.

Acts 1:3 To whom also he shewed himself alive after his passion by many infallible proofs, being seen of them forty days, and speaking of the things pertaining to the kingdom of God:

Acts 1:9-11 And when he had spoken these things, while they beheld, he was taken up; and a cloud received him out of their sight. **10** And while they looked stedfastly toward heaven as he went up, behold, two men stood by them in white apparel; **11** Which also said, Ye men of Galilee, why stand ye gazing up into heaven? this same Jesus, which is taken up from you into heaven, shall so come in like manner as ye have seen him go into heaven.

THERE IS MORE PROOF OF JESUS AS TO WHO HE WAS, WHY HE CAME, AND HIS SOON COMING AGAIN THAN THE CLAIM THAT ANY OF US EVER EXISTED. BELIEVE IT, BE SAVED, AND ENJOY HIS BLESSINGS FOR ALL ETERNITY.

CHAPTER 6
SIN AND SALVATION

I JOHN 3:4. SIN IS TRANSGRESSION AGAINST THE LAW. A SINNER IS ONE WHO PRACTICES LAWLESSNESS. IT IS MISSING THE STANDARD ORDAINED BY GOD, NOT US. IT IS WICKEDNESS IN THE SIGHT OF GOD. ALL UNRIGHTEOUSNESS IS SIN. IT IS REBELLION AGAINST GOD.

1 John 3:4 Whosoever committeth sin transgresseth also the law: for sin is the transgression of the law.

ROMANS 3:23. THE BIBLE TEACHES CLEARLY THAT ALL OF US ARE SINNERS AND COME SHORT OF THE GLORY OF GOD. IF YOU AND I ATTEMPTED TO RUN A RACE WITH A SPEEDING CAR, YOU WOULD RUN A LOT FASTER THAN ME, BUT YOU, TOO, WOULD BE LEFT IN THE DUST. WE BOTH WOULD FALL (SHORT).

Romans 3:23 For all have sinned, and come short of the glory of God;

1 JOHN 1:8, 10. MANY PEOPLE TODAY (ESPECIALLY AS TIME DRAWS TO A CLOSE) THINK THEY DO NOT COMMIT SIN. THEY THINK THEY LIVE WITHIN WHAT THE LAW ALLOWS AND DEMANDS. THIS TYPE OF THINKING BLINDS US TO GOD'S TRUTH.

GOD SAYS "WE DECEIVE OURSELVES, AND THE TRUTH IS NOT IN US." WE ARE IN FACT CALLING GOD A LIAR, AND HIS TRUTH <u>IS NOT</u> IN US.

> *1 John 1:8, 10.* **8** If we say that we have no sin, we deceive ourselves, and the truth is not in us. *10* If we say that we have not sinned, we make him a liar, and his word is not in us.

JAMES 2:10. GOD'S STANDARD IS COMPLETE RIGHTEOUSNESS. IT TAKES ONLY <u>ONE</u> SIN TO MAKE US SINNERS. THROUGH GOD'S EYES WE ARE <u>ALL</u> GUILTY.

> *James 2:10* For whosoever shall keep the whole law, and yet offend in one point, he is guilty of all.

MATTHEW 5:28. JESUS SAID, "THAT WHOSOEVER LOOKETH ON A WOMAN TO LUST AFTER HER HATH COMMITTED ADULTERY WITH HER ALREADY IN HIS HEART." GOD SETS A VERY HIGH STANDARD FOR DEFINING SIN. IF WE VIOLATE GOD'S LAW (EVEN IN OUR THOUGHTS) IT IS SIN. THE FACT THAT WE ARE ALL SINNERS <u>CAN NOT BE DENIED.</u>

> *Matthew 5:28* But I say unto you, That whosoever looketh on a woman to lust after her hath committed adultery with her already in his heart.

CHAPTER 6: SIN AND SALVATION

JAMES 1:13-15. WE CAN'T BLAME GOD FOR BEING TEMPTED. HE CAN'T BE TEMPTED. NEITHER DOES HE TEMPT ANYONE. WE ARE TEMPTED BY OUR OWN LUST. IT IS ALWAYS ENTIRELY OUR FAULT. BLAMING OTHERS OR CIRCUMSTANCES DOES NOT CHANGE TRUTH.

LUST, WHEN CONCEIVED, LEADS TO SIN, AND FINALLY DEATH. THIS IS THE SECOND DEATH; ETERNALLY SEPARATED FROM GOD IN AN AWFUL PLACE OF ETERNAL TORMENT.

> ***James 1:13-15*** *Let no man say when he is tempted, I am tempted of God: for God cannot be tempted with evil, neither tempteth he any man:* ***14*** *But every man is tempted, when he is drawn away of his own lust, and enticed.* ***15*** *Then when lust hath conceived, it bringeth forth sin: and sin, when it is finished, bringeth forth death.*

MATTHEW 13:24-25, 28, 30, 37-40. JESUS SPOKE A PARABLE ABOUT THE KINGDOM OF HEAVEN BEING LIKENED TO A MAN SOWING GOOD SEED IN HIS FIELD. WHILE HE SLEPT HIS ENEMY SOWED TARES (OR WEEDS) AMONG HIS WHEAT. BOTH WHEAT AND WEEDS SPRANG UP.

JESUS INTERPRETED THE PARABLE SAYING THE SOWER IS THE SON OF MAN; THE FIELD IS THE WORLD; THE GOOD SEED

IS THE CHILDREN OF THE KINGDOM; THE TARES ARE THE CHILDREN OF THE WICKED ONE. THE WICKED ONE IS THE <u>DEVIL.</u>

THE DEVIL IS CALLED SATAN, ABADDON, BEELZEBUB, BELIAL, APOLLYON, THE PRINCE OF DEVILS, AND THE PRINCE AND POWER OF THE AIR. HE IS THE ENEMY OF GOD, THE CHURCH, THE BIBLE, AND ALL PEOPLE. HIS DESIRE IS TO TURN EVERYONE AWAY FROM GOD BY ENTICING THEM TO SIN AND DRIVING THEM AWAY FROM GOD AND HIS RIGHTEOUSNESS. REMEMBER HE IS A LIAR AND A DECEIVER. DON'T BE TRAPPED BY HIS CARROTS. HE WILL LEAD MANY TO THE FIRE OF HELL. HIS DESIRE FOR CHRISTIANS IS TO KILL OUR TESTIMONY AND OUR DESIRE TO <u>REALLY</u> SERVE GOD.

Matthew 13:24-25 *Another parable put he forth unto them, saying, The kingdom of heaven is likened unto a man which sowed good seed in his field:* ***25*** *But while men slept, his enemy came and sowed tares among the wheat, and went his way.*

Matthew 13:28 *He said unto them, An enemy hath done this. The servants said unto him, Wilt thou then that we go and gather them up?*

Matthew 13:30 *Let both grow together until the harvest: and in the time of harvest I will say to the*

CHAPTER 6: SIN AND SALVATION

reapers, Gather ye together first the tares, and bind them in bundles to burn them: but gather the wheat into my barn.

***Matthew 13:37-40** He answered and said unto them, He that soweth the good seed is the Son of man; **38** The field is the world; the good seed are the children of the kingdom; but the tares are the children of the wicked one; **39** The enemy that sowed them is the devil; the harvest is the end of the world; and the reapers are the angels. **40** As therefore the tares are gathered and burned in the fire; so shall it be in the end of this world.*

1 PETER 5:8. WE ARE WARNED TO BE SOBER AND VIGILANT BECAUSE THE DEVIL WILL INTOXICATE OUR SOUL WITH SIN. HE STALKS US LIKE A HUNGRY LION. HIS GOAL IS TO DEVOUR. HE IS A LIAR, DECEIVER, MURDERER, PERVERTER OF THE SCRIPTURE, HINDERS THE GOSPEL, WORKS LYING WONDERS, AND IS THE PRINCE AND POWER OF THIS WORLD. DON'T LET THE DEVIL CATCH (OR TEMPT) YOU. IF HE EVER GETS A HOLD, ONLY THE BLOOD OF CHRIST WILL SET YOU FREE.

***1 Peter 5:8** Be sober, be vigilant; because your adversary the devil, as a roaring lion, walketh about, seeking whom he may devour:*

ARE YOU READY?

I CORINTHIANS 10:13. GOOD NEWS! GOD IS FAITHFUL. GOD KNOWS EXACTLY HOW MUCH TEMPTATION EACH OF US CAN TAKE. HE ALWAYS MAKES SURE WE HAVE A WAY TO ESCAPE. OUR PROBLEM IS MANY TIMES WE CHOOSE NOT TO ESCAPE, AND WE GIVE IN TO THE DEVIL AND HIS DEMONS AND/OR TO OUR OWN LUSTS. THE CHOICE IS OURS ALONE, TO SIN OR NOT TO SIN.

1 Corinthians 10:13 There hath no temptation taken you but such as is common to man: but God is faithful, who will not suffer you to be tempted above that ye are able; but will with the temptation also make a way to escape, that ye may be able to bear it.

MARK 7:20-23. JESUS SAID ANY EVIL COMING FROM OUR MIND OR HEART IS SIN. THESE SINS ARE <u>NOT</u> THE OUTWARD COMPLETION OF OUR THOUGHTS, THEY ARE THE REBELLIOUS THOUGHTS IN OUR HEART THAT ARE CONTRARY TO GOD'S PERFECT RIGHTOUSNESS.

Mark 7:20-23 And he said, That which cometh out of the man, that defileth the man. 21 For from within, out of the heart of men, proceed evil thoughts, adulteries, fornications, murders, 22 Thefts, covetousness, wickedness, deceit, lasciviousness, an evil eye, blasphemy, pride, foolishness: 23 All

CHAPTER 6: SIN AND SALVATION

these evil things come from within, and defile the man.

JEREMIAH 17:9. SIN IS LIKE A DISEASE IN OUR HEART, DECEITFUL, WICKED, AND CORRUPT. IT IS SELF-MADE WITHIN OURSELVES. THIS <u>SO-CALLED</u> DISEASE IS TREATABLE AND IS 100% CURABLE. LET IT FESTER AND IT WILL GROW LIKE A CANCER. THE CURE (ONLY CURE) IS THROUGH THE BLOOD OF JESUS CHRIST. SEEK HIM. HE HAS THE CURE.

***Jeremiah 17:9** The heart is deceitful above all things, and desperately wicked: who can know it?*

1 JOHN 1:9. HOW DO WE GET OUR HEART CLEANSED FROM SINS? CONFESS THEM TO JESUS.

TRUSTING JESUS CHRIST WITH ALL OUR HEART IS THE <u>ONLY</u> CURE FOR THIS DREADFUL DISEASE.

***1 John 1:9** If we confess our sins, he is faithful and just to forgive us our sins, and to cleanse us from all unrighteousness.*

LUKE 5:32. JESUS WANTS TO SAVE US. HE SAID REPENT. REPENTANCE IS UNDERSTANDING OUR GUILT AND CHANGING OUR MIND FROM EVIL TO GOOD, ALONG WITH A TOTAL COMMITMENT TO TURNING FROM OUR SINFUL WORLDLY WAYS AND FOLLOWING JESUS BY STRIVING TO CONFORM TO HIS RIGHTEOUSNESS.

Luke 5:32 *I came not to call the righteous, but sinners to repentance.*

ROMANS 10:9,10. WE CONFESS WITH OUR MOUTH WHAT WE BELIEVE IN OUR HEART. BELIEVE THAT JESUS IS OUR LORD AND SAVIOUR, THEN "THOU SHALT BE SAVED." CONFESSION TO GOD MEANS AGREEING WITH HIM CONCERNING HIS VERDICT, GUILTY. WE MUST CONFESS OUR GUILT AND TOTALLY PUT OUR TRUST IN JESUS AS OUR ONLY CURE. WHAT SAVES US IS NOT OUR MOUTH, BUT BELIEVING IN OUR HEART. BELIEVING MEANS TO HAVE FAITH. THAT IS TO BE FIRMLY PERSUADED, TURN FROM OUR SINFUL WAYS, AND FOLLOW JESUS. HEAD AND HEART KNOWLEDGE ARE TWO DIFFERENT THINGS. FOR EXAMPLE: PEOPLE LOOK UP AND BELIEVE AN AIRPLANE CAN FLY, BUT, YOU WOULD HAVE TO HOG-TIE SOME TO GET THEM ON THE AIRPLANE. THEY WILL <u>NOT</u> BE PERSUADED CONCERNING THER SAFETY. THEY HAVE A HEAD KNOWLEDGE, <u>NOT</u> A HEART KNOWLEDGE.

Romans 10:9-10 That if thou shalt confess with thy mouth the Lord Jesus, and shalt believe in thine heart that God hath raised him from the dead, thou shalt be saved. 10 For with the heart man believeth unto righteousness; and with the mouth confession is made unto salvation.

CHAPTER 6: SIN AND SALVATION

ROMANS 5:8. COMMENDETH MEANS DEMONSTRATES OR DISPLAYS. GOD LOVED US SO MUCH THAT HE DISPLAYED HIS LOVE BY ALLOWING HIS ONLY SON TO BE CRUCIFIED FOR <u>ONE</u> PURPOSE; TO SAVE SINNERS LIKE YOU AND ME.

***Romans 5:8.** But God commendeth his love toward us, in that, while we were yet sinners, Christ died for us.*

JOHN 3:18. WE HAVE A CHOICE. WE CAN ACCCEPT THE PAYMENT MADE AND BE SAVED, OR WE CAN REJECT GOD'S PAYMENT AND STAY IN OUR "CONDEMNED ALREADY" STATE.

***John 3:18** He that believeth on him is not condemned: but he that believeth not is condemned already, because he hath not believed in the name of the only begotten Son of God.*

ISAIAH 59:1-2. GOD IS ALWAYS READY TO ANSWER PRAYER. HIS REACH IS INFINITE. HE REACHES OUT TO US. – HE STANDS AT THE DOOR AND KNOCKS. – IF ANYONE WILL OPEN HE WILL COME IN. – OUR PROBLEM IS THAT WE BAR THE DOOR WITH OUR SINS. HOW <u>CAN</u> HE ENTER IN IF OUR DESIRE IS TO KEEP HIM OUT? NEITHER IS GOD'S EAR SO HEAVY THAT HE CAN NOT HEAR. IT IS OUR EARS WHICH WE

INTENTIONALLY STOP UP WHEN HE SPEAKS. HOW CAN WE HEAR?

OUR INIQUITIES ARE A CRIMINAL ACT TOWARD GOD. THEY BUILD A WALL BETWEEN US AND GOD THAT OUR PRAYERS CAN'T PENETRATE. "TEAR DOWN THAT WALL." OUR SINS ARE SO AWFUL IN GOD'S EYES THAT HE HIDES HIS FACE FROM US AND WILL NOT HEAR OUR PRAYERS.

> *Isaiah 59:1-2* *Behold, the LORD'S hand is not shortened, that it cannot save; neither his ear heavy, that it cannot hear:* ***2*** *But your iniquities have separated between you and your God, and your sins have hid his face from you, that he will not hear.*

2 PETER 3:9. GOD'S DESIRE IS TO FELLOWSHIP WITH MAN. HE IS LONGSUFFERING TOWARD US ALL. THE PRAYER HE WANTS TO HEAR FROM A LOST PERSON IS ONE OF REPENTANCE: A CHANGING OF OUR MIND BY TURNING AWAY FROM OUR LIFE OF SIN AND EARNESTLY SEEKING A POSITIVE RELATIONSHIP WITH GOD AND TOWARD GOD.

> ***2 Peter 3:9*** *The Lord is not slack concerning his promise, as some men count slackness; but is longsuffering to us-ward, not willing*

CHAPTER 6: SIN AND SALVATION

that any should perish, but that all should come to repentance.

EPHESIANS 2:8, 9. GRACE IS WHAT GOD DOES FOR US, NOT WHAT WE DO FOR GOD. IT'S UNEARNED AND UNMERITED FAVOR UPON MAN AS A FREE GIFT READY FOR THE TAKING. IT CAN ONLY BE RECEIVED BY GRACE THROUGH FAITH. FAITH IS TRUSTING. YOU CAN'T SEE IT, FEEL IT, OR TOUCH IT, BUT YOU KNOW ITS TRUE. THERE IS ABSOLUTELY NOTHING WE DO OR COULD POSSIBLY DO TO EARN SO GREAT A GIFT. THIS GIFT IS ALREADY PAID FOR BY THE BLOOD OF JESUS CHRIST. WE EITHER ACCEPT THIS GIFT AND RECEIVE ETERNAL SALVATION, OR WE REFUSE IT AND BE DAMNED FOREVER.

***Ephesians 2:8-9** For by grace are ye saved through faith; and that not of yourselves: it is the gift of God: **9** Not of works, lest any man should boast.*

JOHN 3:16. THE LOVE OF GOD IS BEYOND OUR ABILITY TO COMPREHEND. HE GAVE HIS ONLY SON, ALLOWING HIM TO DIE A HORRIBLE DEATH FOR ONLY ONE PURPOSE; TO SAVE SINNERS LIKE YOU AND ME. BELIEVETH IN THE GREEK MEANS TO HAVE FAITH, COMMIT, BE FIRMLY PERSUADED, TRUST, DEPEND ON. IN OTHER WORDS, TURNING AWAY FROM THE WORLD OF SIN AND RELYING TOTALLY ON JESUS AND LIVING FOR HIM.

ARE YOU READY?

> ***John 3:16*** *For God so loved the world, that he gave his only begotten Son, that whosoever believeth in him should not perish, but have everlasting life.*

ROMANS 10:9-12. CONFESSING AND BELIEVING IN ONE'S HEART IS WHAT A LOT OF PEOPLE MISS. THEY SAY A PRAYER BELIEVING IN THEIR HEAD, NOT THEIR HEART. CONFESSING SIN IN THE GREEK MEANS TO ACKNOWLEDGE, ADMIT, WITHDRAW, AND REMOVE. THAT IS, WE AGREE WITH JESUS THAT HE PAID FOR OUR SINS ON THE CROSS AND THAT WE HAVE HEARTFELT REPENTANCE FOR OUR SINS. JESUS PAID IT ALL! CONFESSING A TRUTH THAT JESUS PAID FOR YOUR SIN DEBT WON'T SAVE ANYONE. EVEN SATAN CONFESSES THAT. YOU MUST BELIEVE IN YOUR HEART. BELIEVING IMPLIES THAT ALL HE SAID IN HIS INSTRUCTIONS AND COMMANDMENTS YOU WILL DO TO THE BEST OF YOUR ABILITY. THAT IS TO DIE TO SELF AND LIVE FOR HIM. OLD THINGS ARE PASSED AWAY, AND ALL THINGS BECOME NEW. (HAS THERE BEEN A CHANGE IN YOUR LIFE? WITH THE HEART MAN BELIEVETH UNTO RIGHTEOUSNESS, NOT WITH THE HEAD.)

> ***Romans 10:9-12*** *That if thou shalt confess with thy mouth the Lord Jesus, and shalt believe in thine heart that God hath raised him from the*

CHAPTER 6: SIN AND SALVATION

*dead, thou shalt be saved. **10** For with the heart man believeth unto righteousness; and with the mouth confession is made unto salvation. **11** For the scripture saith, Whosoever believeth on him shall not be ashamed. **12** For there is no difference between the Jew and the Greek: for the same Lord over all is rich unto all that call upon him.*

ROMANS 10:13. THROUGHOUT THE BIBLE, GOD MAKES SALVATION CLEAR AND SIMPLE. WE HAVE A CHOICE. IF YOU HAVE NOT ACCEPTED GOD'S FREE GIFT OF ETERNAL LIFE... DO IT NOW! BELIEVE IN YOUR <u>HEART</u> AND THOU SHALL BE SAVED. (IT IS LATER THAN YOU THINK!)

***Romans 10:13** For whosoever shall call upon the name of the Lord shall be saved.*

2 CORINTHIANS 5:17; GALATIANS 4:7; JOHN 14:15-17; PHILIPPIANS 4:7. WHEN YOU REPENT OF YOUR SIN AND TRUST CHRIST AS YOUR LORD AND SAVIOUR, YOU HAVE IN FACT BEEN RE-CREATED INTO A NEW PERSON. YOU ARE BORN AGAIN. YOU BECOME A SON (OR DAUGHTER) OF GOD AND A JOINT HEIR WITH JESUS CHRIST. GOD GIVES YOU THE HOLY SPIRIT TO LIVE INSIDE YOU AND YOU ARE THEN IN UNION WITH GOD, JESUS, AND THE HOLY SPIRIT. OLD THINGS ARE PASSED AWAY AND ALL

THINGS BECOME NEW. LIVING FOR THE WORLD OF SIN IS NO LONGER YOUR DESIRE. THINGS (SIN) THAT MAY APPEAL TO THE FLESH AND OFFER TEMPORARY PLEASURE WILL BE RESISTED. JOY AND HAPPINESS (IN THE LORD) THAT PASSES ALL UNDERSTANDING WILL FILL YOUR HEART. IT DOES NOT MEAN THAT YOU WON'T HAVE TRIALS AND TRIBULATIONS, BUT AS YOU LIVE THROUGH THEM BY APPLYING GOD'S WORD YOU WILL GROW AND MATURE IN YOUR CHRISTIAN LIFE. IF A DEFINITE CHANGE DOES NOT OCCUR, YOU NEED TO CHECK UP TO ASSURE YOU HAVE ACCEPTED CHRIST IN YOUR HEART AND <u>NOT</u> JUST YOUR HEAD. DO IT NOW!

__2 Corinthians 5:17__ Therefore if any man be in Christ, he is a new creature: old things are passed away; behold, all things are become new.

__Galatians 4:7__ Wherefore thou art no more a servant, but a son; and if a son, then an heir of God through Christ.

__John 14:15-17__ If ye love me, keep my commandments. __16__ And I will pray the Father, and he shall give you another Comforter, that he may abide with you for ever; __17__ Even the Spirit of truth; whom the world cannot receive, because it seeth him not, neither knoweth him: but ye know

CHAPTER 6: SIN AND SALVATION

him; for he dwelleth with you, and shall be in you.

Philippians 4:7 *And the peace of God, which passeth all understanding, shall keep your hearts and minds through Christ Jesus.*

I JOHN 1:9; I JOHN 2:1, 2. SOME PEOPLE WILL SAY: "WAIT A MINUTE, I AM SAVED, I HAVE ETERNAL LIFE, AND CAN'T BE LOST. I'LL LIVE MY LIFE THE WAY I WANT TO WITHOUT FEAR OF EVER BEING REJECTED." THIS CAN'T BE DONE. AS CHILDREN OF GOD AND JOINT HEIRS WITH JESUS CHRIST WE ARE MEMBERS OF GOD'S FAMILY. WE DO HAVE GOD'S LOVE. WE ARE HIS CHILDREN AND WILL BE TREATED AS A CHILD OF GOD, A FAMILY MEMBER. AS NEWBORN CHRISTIANS, (JUST LIKE A CHILD) WE WILL SIN. JESUS SAID DON'T SIN, BUT WHEN WE DO WE HAVE JESUS OUR ADVOCATE WHO SITS ON THE RIGHT HAND OF GOD PLEADING OUR CASE. IF SATAN SAYS LOOK AT THAT SIN, JESUS WILL SAY IT'S UNDER THE BLOOD, FORGIVEN, AND FORGOTTEN. HE WILL NEVER LOSE A CASE.

1 John 1:9 *If we confess our sins, he is faithful and just to forgive us our sins, and to cleanse us from all unrighteousness.*

1 John 2:1-2 *My little children, these things write I unto you, that ye sin not. And if any man sin, we have* *an advocate with the Father, Jesus Christ the righteous:* ***2*** *And he is the propitiation for our sins: and not for ours only, but also for the sins of the whole world.*

HEBREWS 12:5-11, 1 CORINTHIANS 11:30. ONE COULD AGAIN SAY I'LL LIVE LIKE I PLEASE BECAUSE MY ADVOCATE WILL ALWAYS WIN, BUT THAT IS NOT POSSIBLE. IF YOU <u>ARE</u> SAVED YOU WILL WANT TO PLEASE YOUR FATHER, AND LISTEN, AND OBEY ALL HIS COMMANDMENTS. A <u>CHRISTIAN</u> CAN REBEL AGAINST GOD AND LIVE IN HABITUAL SIN, BUT HE <u>CAN'T</u> GET AWAY WITH IT. FOR EXAMPLE, IF YOU DEFILE YOUR BODY BY SMOKING OR DRINKING YOU MAY END UP WITH CANCER, EMPHYSEMA, HEART PROBLEMS, AND MANY OTHER DISEASES, NOT TO MENTION A BROKEN FAMILY. GOD SAYS HE WILL CHASTEN AND SCOURGE <u>EVERY</u> SON HE RECEIVES BECAUSE YOU ARE A SON (OR DAUGHTER). CHASTENING CAN TAKE MANY FORMS SUCH AS GUILT, CONVICTION, SOME SICKNESS, WEAKNESS, AND EVEN AN EARLY DEATH. HE SAID IF HE DOESN'T CHASTEN YOU, YOU ARE BASTARDS AND <u>NOT</u> SONS. GOD WILL CHASTEN HIS OWN. THAT IS WHY A PROFESSED CHRISTIAN (NOT SAVED) APPEARS TO LIVE FOR SATAN WITH APPARENTLY NO VISIBLE CONSEQUENCES. HE IS A BASTARD AND NOT A SON. HIS JUDGMENT IS AT THE GREAT WHITE THRONE JUDGMENT.

CHAPTER 6: SIN AND SALVATION

Hebrews 12:5-11 *And ye have forgotten the exhortation which speaketh unto you as unto children, My son, despise not thou the chastening of the Lord, nor faint when thou art rebuked of him:* **6** *For whom the Lord loveth he chasteneth, and scourgeth every son whom he receiveth.* **7** *If ye endure chastening, God dealeth with you as with sons; for what son is he whom the father chasteneth not?* **8** *But if ye be without chastisement, whereof all are partakers, then are ye bastards, and not sons.* **9** *Furthermore we have had fathers of our flesh which corrected us, and we gave them reverence: shall we not much rather be in subjection unto the Father of spirits, and live?* **10** *For they verily for a few days chastened us after their own pleasure; but he for our profit, that we might be partakers of his holiness.* **11** *Now no chastening for the present seemeth to be joyous, but grievous: nevertheless afterward it yieldeth the peaceable fruit of righteousness unto them which are exercised thereby.*

1 Corinthians 11:30 *For this cause many are weak and sickly among you, and many sleep.*

1 JOHN 1:4-7. NO ONE CAN HAVE A FULL LIFE OF JOY WITHOUT WALKING IN

THE SPIRITUAL PATHWAY OF THE LIGHT OF GOD. WALKING IN HIS LIGHT WILL KEEP YOU FROM STRAYING OFF THE PATHWAY INTO THE DARKNESS OF SIN. WE CAN HAVE TRUE FELLOWSHIP WITH GOD AS WELL AS OTHERS BY WALKING IN HIS LIGHT. WHICH PATH WILL YOU CHOOSE? [REPENT, BELIEVE, CALL, TRUST, AND BE SAVED.]

> *1 John 1:4-7 And these things write we unto you, that your joy may be full. 5 This then is the message which we have heard of him, and declare unto you, that God is light, and in him is no darkness at all. 6 If we say that we have fellowship with him, and walk in darkness, we lie, and do not the truth: 7 But if we walk in the light, as he is in the light, we have fellowship one with another, and the blood of Jesus Christ his Son cleanseth us from all sin.*

2 CORINTHIANS 6:2. IN THIS VERSE, PAUL EMPHASIZES TO GET SAVED TODAY! YOU MAY NOT HAVE A TOMORROW! IT IS LATER THAN YOU THINK!

> *2 Corinthians 6:2 (For he saith, I have heard thee in a time accepted, and in the day of salvation have I succoured thee: behold, now is the accepted time; behold, now is the day of salvation.)*

INDEX

1,000 YEARS 49, 52
1,500 MILES 103
300 YEARS 118
ABANDON 55
ABANDONED 57
ABILITY.......26, 31, 36, 82, 89, 90, 121, 139, 140
ABODE 101
ACCEPT 55, 139
ACCEPTABLE .... .22, 23, 63
ACCEPTED....3, 114, 141, 142
ACCEPTING 109
ACCEPTS 24
ACCESS 103
ACCOUNTED 55
ACHIEVE 23
ACKNOWLEDGE 140
ACQUIRE 33
ACT...........119, 138
ADAM................ 74
ADMIT 140
ADOPTION 127
ADORE 31
ADORNED 101
ADULTERY 130
ADVOCATE 124, 143, 144
AFFAIRS 40

AGAINST........5, 18, 51, 73, 81, 101, 129, 144
AGE 17, 109
AGES 40
AGREE 140
AGREEING 136
AGREEMENT . 40, 94
AIR............47, 80, 132, 183
AIRPLANE 136
ALLEGIANCE 31
ALLOWS 129
ALMIGHTY........ 103
AMBASSADOR 99
AMERICA...25, 109, 184
AMERICANS 90
ANGEL.. 29, 49, 111
ANGRY 68
ANIMALS.... 67, 105
ANTICHRIST 41
ANTIGOD 41
ANTISPIRIT 41
ANYONE......67, 90, 131, 137, 140
ANYTHING...19, 33, 86, 90, 103, 105
APOLLYON 132
APPEAL 71, 142
APPETITE.......... 110

APPLICATION ... 32, 64
APPLYING 142
APPOINTED 37
ARMOR............... 81
ARREST 117
ARTIFICIAL...... 103
ARTIFICIALLY.... 15
ASCEND 101
ASCENDED 124
ASCENSION 117, 125, 126
ASHAMED.....13, 25, 34
ASSEMBLY ... 41, 42
ASSURE............ 142
ASSURED 55
ATLANTA JOURNAL 38
ATMOSPHERIC ... 97
ATTEND............... 26
ATTITUDE 23, 30
AUTHORITY.34, 55, 71, 85
AVOID.... 26, 49, 66
AWFUL.........67, 79, 131, 138
BABE............ 27, 28
BABY................... 27
BAD..........9, 13, 18, 35, 36
BAG................... 116
BALLPARK........ 100
BAPTIST....89, 184, 185
BAPTIZED...........35
BAR 137
BASTARDS........144
BEAST....15, 41, 47, 49, 54
BEAUTY 105
BEELZEBUB 132
BEG 21, 27
BEGGAR........ 91, 93
BEGINNING........47, 72, 97
BEHIND 106
BELIEF 50
BELIEVE5, 9, 13, 15, 18, 25, 31, 36, 38, 53, 67, 90, 97, 119, 128, 136, 140, 141, 146
BELIEVING. 54, 125, 136, 140
BENEFITTED 30
BESEECH 21
BEST..... 26, 36, 140
BETHLEHEM EPHRATAH.....112
BETRAY 117
BETTER........65, 80, 103, 116
BIBLE5, 10, 11, 18, 19, 21, 26-28, 32, 34, 37, 38, 67,

INDEX

72, 84, 95, 109, 122, 129, 132, 141
BIRDS........ 97, 105
BIRTH.............. 112
BITTERNESS 119
BLAME 131
BLEED 121
BLESSED 46, 114
BLESSINGS 109, 128
BLOOD...19, 45, 56, 64, 83, 98, 121, 133, 135, 139, 143
BLOTTED OUT 19
BODIES........20, 22, 60, 63
BODY.......5, 41, 98, 123, 144
BONDAGE 19, 20
BONE 121
BOOK.....3, 5, 9, 15, 24, 43, 58, 79, 104
BOOKS..10, 58, 173
BORE 118
BORN.....12, 27, 29, 111, 112, 116, 141, 183
BOTTOM..... 69, 105
BOTTOMLESS PIT 49
BOUGHT............. 19
BOW 45, 57

BOWING............. 57
BOX.................... 90
BREADTH 103
BRIDE 101
BRIMSTONE 78
BROKEN 144
BROTHER 68
BROTHERS...45, 69, 95
BRUISE 109
BRUISED 118
BUILD .. 14, 15, 138
BUILT................. 97
BURIED 119
BURN 81
BURNED 15, 67
CALL......41, 75, 97, 146
CALLING 68, 130
CALVARY............ 53
CANAANITES...... 67
CANCER.... 135, 144
CAPABILITY 22
CAPABLE 51
CAPERNAUM....... 87
CAR 93, 129
CARES 98, 127
CARROTS.......... 132
CASE 124, 143
CAST......37, 39, 43, 47, 49, 54, 60, 61, 79, 82, 83
CATCH 25, 133
CELESTIAL . 97, 101

149

CENTER 75, 77, 103
CENTURIES 25
CENTURY 10, 62
CHAIN 49
CHAINED 51, 52
CHAINS 39, 73
CHAINS OF DARKNESS 39, 73
CHANGE...131, 140, 142
CHANGING ...... .135, 138
CHARACTER 13
CHASTEN 144
CHECK 142
CHILD 111, 143
CHILDREN 3, 9, 19, 20, 67, 90, 132, 143
CHOICE 66, 134, 137, 141
CHOOSE 73, 134, 146
CHRIST5, 7, 9, 11, 12-15, 19, 23, 25-28, 32, 35-37, 40-42, 44, 45, 50, 51, 54-56, 64, 66, 79, 83, 85, 88, 90, 95, 96, 98, 102, 105, 109, 118, 119, 127, 133, 135, 139, 141, 143

CHRISTIAN....9, 18, 25, 29, 81, 142, 144, 183
CHRISTIANS..5, 12, 20, 23-25, 62, 99, 132, 143
CHURCH...5, 17, 22, 25, 26, 29, 41, 42, 51, 94, 106, 132, 184, 185
CITIZENSHIP 98
CITY 102-104
CLASSIC ANSWER 29
CLEANSED 135
CLEAR 29, 105, 141
CLOSE 17, 25, 122, 129
CLOTHES 93, 121
CLOUD 102
CO-EQUAL 56
COMING 11, 15, 64, 80, 85, 107, 110, 125, 128, 134
COMMAND 27, 35
COMMANDED 19, 33, 86
COMMANDMENT 62, 64
COMMANDMENTS 9, 19, 32, 34, 36, 63, 100, 140, 144
COMMENDETH .. 137

INDEX

COMMISSION.... 18, 62
COMMIT............ 54, 129, 139
COMMITMENT .. 135
COMMITTED.26, 55, 58, 93, 120, 130
COMMUNION 42
COMPARTMENT.. 77
COMPARTMENTS 75
COMPASSION ... 45, 69, 93, 94, 95
COMPEL 35
COMPLACENT..... 99
COMPLETE...40, 71, 103, 130
COMPLETION ... 134
COMPOUNDED . 119
COMPREHEND.. 139
COMPUTERS....... 25
CONCERNED....... 62
CONDEMNED.... 137
CONDUCT..... 13, 24
CONFESS......29, 57, 135, 136
CONFESSING ... 140
CONFESSION ... 136
CONFIDENT 98
CONFORM 135
CONFORMED 22
CONFUSED 97
CONQUERER 125
CONSCIENCE 89
CONSCIOUS 61

CONSEQUENCES 144
CONSIDER...11, 13, 53, 93
CONSTRAINED ... 29
CONTAIN.... 58, 101
CONTAMINATE . 105
CONTINUE.......... 32
CONTRARY 134
CONTROL 51, 56
CONVERSATION . 98
CONVICTING 22
CORRUPT 135
COUNTERFEIT 42
COUNTRIES....... 25, 184
COUNTRY 5, 99
CREATE 9, 15, 67
CREATED..7, 31, 67, 72, 74, 97, 141
CREATURES........ 15
CRIMINAL 138
CRIMINALS 67
CROSS....23, 24, 53, 90, 120-122, 125, 140
CROWN 121
CRUCIFIED...... 119, 120, 122, 123, 137
CRUCIFY 84
CRY 27
CRYING 102
CRYSTAL 105

151

CUBE 103
CUP 42
CURABLE 135
CURE .. 83, 135, 136
CURRENT EVENTS 17
CURSORY 109
DAILY 23, 24, 25
DAMNABLE 37
DAMNATION 85
DAMNED 139
DANGER 68
DANIEL 42, 110
DARKNESS ... 73, 90, 146
DAVID 94, 114
DAY 11, 25, 37, 38, 45, 54, 61, 78, 80, 93, 95, 102, 104, 114, 125
DEAD 22, 38, 55, 67, 113, 124
DEAD BODIES 67
DEATH ... 22, 60, 71, 75, 83, 95, 97, 102, 121, 122, 125, 131, 139, 144
DECEITFUL 135
DECEIVE 130
DECEIVED 65
DECEIVER 81, 132, 133

DEEDS 14, 55
DEFEAT 40
DEFEATED 43, 47
DEFILE 144
DEFINING 130
DEFINITION 13
DEGREE 58, 94, 183
DEGREES .. 7, 58, 67, 81-83, 96
DELIVERANCE 19
DELUSION 106
DEMANDS ... 82, 129
DEMONIC 54
DEMONS 15, 40, 67, 80, 134
DEMONSTRATED 53, 102
DENIED 127, 130
DENIERS 40
DENY 25, 37
DENYING 38, 39, 118
DEPEND 139
DERIVATIVES 11
DESCEND 77
DESCENDED. 74, 125
DESCRIBE 60, 67, 93
DESERVE 58
DESIGNED 97

INDEX

DESIRES....... 9, 27, 29, 90, 132, 137, 138, 142
DESPISED 68
DEVASTATING ... 65
DEVIL....43, 50, 67, 73, 80, 81, 132, 133, 134
DEVOTION 31
DEVOUR..... 85, 133
DEVOURED......... 80
DIE.........23, 37, 96, 110, 139, 140
DIED......25, 44, 69, 74, 91, 121, 122
DIES 98
DILIGENT 33
DIRECT 103
DIRT 31
DISCIPLE.....24, 25, 115, 119, 123
DISCIPLES. 81, 126
DISEASE 135
DISEASES 144
DISOBEDIENCE.. 19
DISOBEYING...... 58
DISPENSATION... 5, 51
DISPLAYS 137
DISTINCT 40, 41
DIVINE 103
DIVING 105
DOERS 27
DOGS 29, 68
DOMINATED 23
DONKEY 114
DOOR 29, 137
DOUBT 51, 109
DOUBTING THOMAS 119
DOUBTS 97
DRAGON............. 41
DREADFUL.. 45, 135
DREAM 90
DRINKING........ 144
DRIPPING 64
DRIVING 132
DRONES 16, 17
DROUGHT......... 105
DUST................. 129
DWELL 102, 125
DWELLING...97, 99, 101
DYING................ 62
EAR 137
EARN................ 139
EARNESTLY 21, 138
EARS 110, 137
EARTH....34, 58, 72, 74, 77, 93, 101, 103, 105, 109, 124
EARTHLY 98
EAT 29, 119
EDEN................. 74
ELECTRONIC DEVICE............ 29

153

EMORY UNIVERSITY.... 38
EMPHASIZES.... 146
EMPHYSEMA 144
EMPTY........ 68, 125
END..........5, 17, 47, 49, 51, 70, 117, 144
ENEMIES.......... 117
ENEMY.......41, 131, 132
ENTER......104, 114, 137
ENTICING 132
ENTREAT............ 21
ENVIRONMENT . 72, 83, 102, 105
ESCAPE5..5, 71, 78, 79, 134
ESTABLISH .. 37, 49
ETERNAL.......41, 45, 55, 60, 61, 67, 78, 79, 96, 99, 131, 139, 141, 143
ETERNALLY..12, 37, 131
ETERNITY....45, 58, 62, 70, 98, 105, 128
EVERLASTING ... 12, 78, 81
EVERYONE...27, 32, 64, 103, 109, 132

EVIL.......47, 49, 55, 86, 120-122, 134, 135
EXAMPLE...15, 136, 144
EXCUSE 26, 89
EXEMPT...............58
EXHAUSTS..........60
EXIST.........98, 102
EXISTENCE.........74
EYES... 11, 130, 138
FACE....25, 31, 105, 138
FACT......89, 94, 98, 110, 118, 122, 130, 141
FAILURE....... 36, 65
FAITH....24, 37, 50, 91, 93, 109, 117, 123, 136, 139
FAITHFUL........9, 21, 134
FALSE....37, 41, 47, 54
FAMILY..24, 27, 34, 127, 143, 144
FATHER..40, 56, 63, 104, 127, 144
FAULT...............131
FAVOR..............139
FEAR 57, 70, 143
FED 27, 34
FEELING...........119

INDEX

FELLOWSHIP .. 138, 146
FENCE STRADDLING .. 44
FIELD 131
FILL 27, 142
FINAL 39, 45, 55, 101, 119
FINGER . 44, 69, 119
FIRE 57, 67, 68, 78, 101, 132
FISH 114
FISHING BOAT . 100
FIVE HUNDRED . 126
FLESH 50, 111, 142
FLOWING 105
FLY 97, 136
FOLLOW 23-25, 52, 73, 99, 136
FOLLOWING . 24, 25, 47, 62, 69, 110, 135
FOOD 68, 93, 114
FOOD SUPPLY .. 114
FOOL 68, 93
FOOLED 43
FORBEAR 116
FORBIDDEN 19
FOREVER 35, 37, 54, 56, 61, 71, 78, 98, 106, 139
FORGIVEN 9, 13, 19, 143
FORGOTTEN 143
FORM 10, 56
FOUNDATION 14, 15
FOUR HUNDRED AND NINETY .. 110
FREE 21, 25, 56, 66, 89, 121, 127, 133, 139, 141
FREEDOM 103
FRIGHTENING ... 13, 36
FRUIT 63, 105
FULFILLED 109, 116, 122
FULL 96, 145
FUTURE 46
GARBAGE DUMP . 67
GARDEN 74, 117
GATES 67, 104
GAVE 24, 25, 66, 82, 89, 119, 125, 139
GEHENNA 67
GENESIS 72, 74, 97, 109
GENTILES ... 39, 113
GETHSEMANE ... 117
GIFT 45, 56, 98, 100, 125, 127, 139, 141
GIFTS 21, 125
GIVE 25, 29, 81, 95, 116, 134

155

GIVES 94, 141
GLORIFIED 63
GLORIFY 15
GLORY...10, 26, 36, 104, 129
GOAL 40, 133
GOD......5, 9-13, 15, 18-23, 26-33, 35-43, 46, 51, 53, 56, 57, 60, 62, 63, 64, 66-68, 72-74, 81-84, 86, 88, 89, 91, 92, 94, 95, 97, 98, 100-103, 105, 106, 109, 111, 113, 118, 121, 124, 127, 129-132, 134, 136-139, 141, 143, 144, 146
GODHEAD 40
GOOD.......9, 13, 18, 21, 23, 27, 36, 83, 91, 99, 120, 131, 134, 135
GOOGLE 16
GOSPEL..25, 88, 90, 93, 133
GOVERN 106
GRACE5 19, 51, 53, 95, 139
GRANTS 98
GRATIFICATION 18

GRAVE 122, 125
GRAVITY 58
GREAT....3, 7, 9, 10, 34, 62, 75, 81, 90, 97, 99, 100, 116, 139
GREEK............ ....13, 14, 24, 33, 34, 69, 98, 114, 117, 139, 140
GRIEFS.............118
GROW 99, 135, 142
GROWLING.........29
GUILTY........55, 58, 130, 136
GULF 75, 94
HABITUAL 144
HADES.................67
HALLELUJAH 121
HAND 28, 119
HANDS 64, 119
HANGED 117
HANGING 120
HAPPINESS 142
HARDSHIP..........23
HARVEST............95
HATE 68, 120
HATED 68
HEAD5.......54, 109, 116, 121, 136, 140, 142
HEALING .. 105, 113
HEAR........9, 68, 69, 86, 137, 138

INDEX

HEARERS 27
HEARING ... 90, 119
HEART......5, 32, 54, 62, 68, 77, 93, 94, 96, 97, 116, 130, 134, 135, 136, 140-142, 144
HEARTFELT 140
HEAVEN.....7, 9, 43, 67, 71-75, 85, 96-99, 101, 106, 117, 124, 126, 127, 131
HEBREW 21, 75
HEBREWS....27, 37, 144
HEIGHT............ 103
HEIR 141
HEIRS......102, 127, 143
HELL........7, 39, 43, 57-60, 67-69, 71, 72, 74, 75, 77-79, 81-83, 85, 86, 91, 93-96, 125, 132
HERESIES 37
HIDE.......55, 57, 80
HIGH....13, 26, 103, 105, 114, 130, 183
HIGHER 99
HIGHEST.......... 114
HILLTOP 97
HINDERS.......... 133
HISTORY....47, 109, 113, 122
HOG-TIE............ 136
HOLINESS 13
HOLY.......5, 18, 22, 26, 29, 35, 36, 40, 53, 56, 63, 70, 99, 109, 111, 118, 127, 141
HOLY GHOST 111
HOLY SPIRIT..... 29, 40, 56, 118, 127, 141
HONOR. 36, 99, 104
HOPE......29, 45, 55, 57, 67
HORRIBLE 139
HOSANNA.......... 114
HOUSE ... 29, 74, 97
HUMAN............... 60
HUMILIATION .. 121
HUNDREDS...... 109, 119
HUNGRY.......80, 93, 133
HUSBAND......... 102
IGNORANCE 26
IMAGE 15, 47
IMAGINE......52, 68, 90, 97, 100, 105, 119
IMAGINED........ 100
IMMANUEL 111

157

IMMATURE... 27, 28
IMPLIES........... 140
IMPLORE............ 21
IMPORTANCE..... 21
IMPORTANT...9, 99, 122
IMPOSSIBLE.... 100
IMPOSTER.......... 13
INCORRUPTIBLE 99
INFALLIBLE..... 127
INFINITE... 19, 137
INFLUENCE.. 40, 54
INHERIT........... 102
INIQUITIES..... 138
INIQUITY.....11, 73, 83, 118
INNOCENT....... 120
INSTANTLY........ 98
INSTRUCTED...... 56
INSTRUCTIONS. 24, 140
INSTRUMENTS... 20
INSULTED........ 120
INTELLIGENT.... 15, 22, 80
INTENTIONALLY 138
INTERCEDE...... 103
INTEREST........... 97
INTERPRETED.. 131
INTOXICATE.... 133
INVISIBLE......... 71
ISRAEL............. 113
JERUSALEM. 67, 101, 103, 112, 114
JESUS........7, 9, 14, 15, 19, 23-27, 31, 34-37, 39, 40, 44, 45, 47, 49-51, 53-58, 61-63, 66-69, 71, 73-75, 77, 78, 81-84, 87-89, 93-99, 102, 103, 105-107, 109, 110-120, 122-125, 127, 128, 130, 131, 134-136, 139-141, 143
JEWS......32, 39, 64, 121
JOINT......102, 127, 141, 143
JOSEPH.... 111, 123
JOY.... 62, 142, 145
JUDAH............... 112
JUDAS...... 115, 116
JUDGE....11, 13, 18, 19, 26, 55, 63, 71, 96
JUDGED...9, 12, 13, 15, 25, 34, 36, 37, 55, 60, 82, 83, 87, 96
JUDGMENT.......7, 9, 11-13, 15, 17, 18,

INDEX

26, 28, 31, 35, 36-39, 45, 58, 64, 68, 87, 144
JUNGLE 80
JUST 9, 25, 27, 33, 34, 44, 47, 69, 80, 82-84, 88, 91, 92, 94, 96, 97, 118, 120, 142, 143
JUSTICE .. 11, 82, 83
KEEP 9, 19, 21, 32, 34-36, 63, 83, 87, 88, 97, 100, 137, 146
KEEPER 115, 185
KEYS 71
KILL 15, 19, 132
KILLED 24
KINGDOM 27, 49, 51, 85, 125, 131, 132
KINGS ... 48, 57, 103
KISS 117
KNEE 57
KNOCKS 137
KNOWLEDGE 5, 9, 10, 27, 33, 34, 54, 74, 88, 112, 116, 136
LADY 82
LAKE 37, 43, 47, 54, 58, 60, 65, 79, 83

LAKE OF FIRE 37, 43, 47, 54, 58, 60, 65, 79, 83
LAMB 103
LAND 101, 109
LANGUAGE ... 21, 60
LASH 121
LAST 10, 43, 109
LATER 45, 118, 119, 120, 122, 141, 146
LAUGH 120
LAW 18, 19, 22, 121, 129, 130
LAWLESSNESS . 129
LEADING 99
LEAVES 105
LEGION 121
LENGTH 103
LIAR 130-133
LIE 19, 97
LIFE 15, 22-24, 44, 45, 54, 58, 73, 79, 97, 98, 104-106, 123, 138, 140-143, 145
LIFETIME ... 55, 119
LIGHT 89, 102, 103, 146
LION 52, 80, 133
LIPS 120
LISTEN 144

LIVE 18, 23, 95, 109, 129, 140, 141, 143, 144
LIVES . 3, 24, 56, 62
LIVING ... 22, 25, 51, 63, 82, 139, 142
LOCATED 97, 112
LOCUSTS 15
LONGSUFFERING 38, 138
LOOKETH 130
LORD 9, 11, 20, 22, 32, 33, 35, 41, 48, 55, 57, 66, 72, 74, 75, 94, 95, 98, 103, 109, 111, 113, 114, 118, 121, 125, 136, 138, 141
LORDS 48, 57
LOSE 24, 143
LOSS 15
LOST 5, 7, 12, 37, 45, 57, 58, 64, 78, 79, 93, 96, 119, 138, 143
LOVE 5, 9, 19, 32, 53, 63, 68, 96, 100, 116, 127, 137, 139, 143
LOVED 9, 65, 68, 137
LOVING 67, 127

LUCIFER 101
LUKEWARM 22
LUST 130, 131
LUSTS 134
MAN 9, 14, 15, 51, 56, 70, 72, 81, 83, 84, 89, 91, 93, 95, 97, 102, 111, 127, 131, 138-140
MANIFEST 14
MANSION ... 98, 100
MARK 26, 47, 60, 82, 106, 134
MARKET 19
MARTYRDOM 25
MARTYRS MIRROR 24
MARVELOUS 114
MASTER 20, 116
MASTERS 86
MATURE 23, 142
MEASURE 103
MEASUREMENT. 110
MEDITATE 26, 33
MEMBER 29, 143
MEMBERS . 127, 143
MERCIES 21
MERCY 37, 94
MESSIAH 110, 114, 116, 118
METAL 121
MILE 30
MILK 27, 28

INDEX

MIMIC 40
MIND 23, 56, 83, 87, 88, 134, 135, 138
MINDS ... 40, 56, 57, 102
MINISTRY 42, 184, 185
MINUTE 143
MIRACLES 87, 113, 115, 120
MISS 44, 53, 140
MISSION 20
MISSIONARY 90
MOCKED 120, 121
MOCKERY 121
MODERN 93, 95, 109
MONTH 105, 117
MONTICELLO, FL. 68, 183
MOON 97
MORAL LAW 68
MORALS 68
MOTIVES 18, 23, 36, 86
MOURN 119
MOUTH 136
MULTIPLY 114
MULTITUDE 113
MURDERER 133
NAILING 121
NAILS 119

NAME ... 79, 89, 111, 114
NAMED 111, 112
NAMES 58, 104
NATION 90, 118
NATIONS 105
NATIVE CHIEF 90
NATURE 51
NAZARETH 87
NEGLECT 99
NEGLIGENCE 26, 29
NEIGHBOR ... 19, 68, 93
NEW 20, 23, 27, 67, 68, 70, 98, 100, 101, 103, 124, 140, 141
NEW TESTAMENT 20, 67, 68, 70
NICODEMUS 27, 123
NIGHT 37, 54, 68, 78, 102
NO HOPE 37, 45, 60, 97, 124
NORTH 101
OBEISANCE 31
OBSERVE 35, 57
OBTAIN 100
OCCUR . 51, 65, 142
OFFICE 99, 184
OLD 2, 20, 22, 64, 67, 69, 75, 98, 112, 140, 141

161

OLD TESTAMENT. 22, 64, 67, 69, 75, 112
OMISSION ... 18, 19
ONE........13, 15, 18, 20, 23-25, 29, 31, 32, 40-42, 56, 62, 68, 71, 72, 75, 81, 83, 86, 89, 91, 93, 95, 105, 109, 118, 121, 122, 129, 130, 132, 137-140, 144, 145, 183
ONLY.....12, 13, 15, 27, 30, 31, 41, 57, 58, 63, 83, 91, 93, 104, 105, 119, 130, 133, 135-137, 139
OPEN........9, 14, 71, 104, 118, 121, 137
OPPORTUNITIES 31
OPPORTUNITY .. 10, 57, 87, 109, 119, 184
OPTION............... 35
ORDAINED 129, 184
OURSELVES......... 18, 23, 63, 130, 135
OUTER DARKNESS 61
OUTWARD........ 134

OWN........5, 11, 24, 29, 32, 68, 81, 93, 123, 124, 131, 134, 144
PAID......13, 19, 56, 105, 116, 139, 140
PAIN 15, 102
PARABLE......30, 58, 131
PARADISE....75, 77, 91, 124
PASSAGES 21
PASSED......98, 140, 141
PASTOR...... 29, 184
PATH 110, 146
PATHWAY......... 146
PAYMENT.....67, 79, 137
PENETRATE 138
PEOPLE....5, 25, 35, 37, 38, 40, 41, 43, 47, 51, 58, 62, 64, 67, 73, 78, 79, 82, 83, 90, 91, 93, 95-97, 102, 106, 111, 113, 114, 116, 120, 129, 132, 136, 140, 143
PERFECT......23, 29, 58, 72, 73, 83, 102, 134

INDEX

PERFECTION 13
PERFECTLY 92, 103
PERFORM 31, 99
PERSECUTION .. 23, 35
PERSON 41, 58, 68, 74, 88, 90, 93, 120, 138, 141
PERSONIFIED 13
PERSUADED 136, 139
PERVERTER 133
PICTURE 80
PIERCED 118
PILATE 84, 120, 123
PLACE 19, 23, 37, 49, 55, 57, 61, 67-69, 73, 75, 77-81, 96, 97, 99, 101, 103, 112, 131
PLAGUE 57
PLEAD 27
PLEADING 143
PLEASE 21, 144
PLEASURE 18, 31, 142
PLEDGED 31
PLURAL. 41, 78, 100
POSITION .. 99, 100
POSITIVE 138
POSSIBLE .. 90, 144
POSTPONE 55
POUND 110
POWER .. 34, 80, 84, 132, 133
POWERFUL 40
PRACTICES 129
PRAISE 36, 114
PRAY 19, 33, 114
PRAYER ... 3, 10, 33, 90, 137, 138, 140
PRAYERS 138
PREACHED 90
PREDICTED 120
PREPARATION 26
PREPARE 97, 106
PREPARED 43, 100, 101, 105, 123
PRESENCE .. 61, 102, 103
PRESENT 22, 98, 115, 185
PRETENDER 13
PRICE 13, 19, 56, 105, 116
PRIDE 116
PRIEST 103, 116
PRIESTS 85, 120
PRINCE 80, 132, 133
PRINTING PRESS. 25
PRIORITY 62
PROBLEM 18, 29, 86, 90, 134, 137

163

PROBLEMS 144
PRODUCE 63
PROFESSOR 38
PROFITED 30
PROMISES 32
PROOF 43, 109, 128
PROPHESIED.... 109
PROPHESIES ... 109, 110, 117, 122
PROPHETS ... 37, 69
PROSTRATE 31
PROVE . 23, 51, 109
PROVERB 62
PUCKER............. 120
PUNISHED...58, 83, 88, 94, 96, 122
PUNISHMENT...... 7, 45, 55, 58, 67, 69, 78, 81-83, 85, 86, 96, 119
PURIFIED. 101, 105
PURITY 69, 105
PURPOSE.....10, 23, 28, 56, 109, 111, 118, 137, 139
QUALITY 81
QUANTITY.... 58, 81
QUESTION.....9, 18, 21, 22, 94, 95
QUESTIONED ... 109
QUOTED 21, 38
RABBI 27
RACA.................. 68

RACE 129
RAISING 113
RAPTURE 17, 22, 51
REACH 137
REACHES 137
REAL......61, 67-69, 71, 77, 79, 81, 89, 96, 97, 109
REAP 62, 84
REBEL.........51, 144
REBELLED... 73, 101
REBELLION. 18, 129
REBELLIOUS..... 134
RECEIVE.......12, 13, 15, 45, 56, 82, 85, 97, 99, 127, 139
RECEIVING....... 100
RECOGNIZE 119
RECOGNIZED...... 57
RECORD 58
REDEEM.....15, 105, 127
REDEEMING.. ....21, 53, 83
REDEMPTION 19, 56, 121
REFLECTION....... 29
REFUSE 88, 95, 139
REFUSED 55
REFUSING 25, 67
REHABILITATION
........................83
REINFORCEMENT 29

INDEX

REJECT...56, 58, 83, 137
REJECTED... ...... 79, 113, 114, 120, 143
REJECTING .. 45, 73
RELATIONSHIP. 97, 138
RELYING 139
REMORSE... 57, 117
REMOVE 140
REMOVED 99
REPENT..50, 66, 87, 90, 95, 135, 141, 146
REPENTANCE 85, 135, 138, 140
REPENTED . 95, 122
REPLACED 99
REPRESENTING . 99
REPUTATION 56
REQUIRED 88
RESIST 50
RESISTED 142
RESPECT 99, 100
RESPONSIBILITY 64, 99, 184
REST 78, 93
RESURRECTION 75, 124, 127
RETURN........57, 97, 106, 185
REVEAL 18, 90
REVEALED.......5, 15, 30, 110
REVEALS......31, 58, 60, 89, 109, 110
REVELATION15, 31, 42, 43, 46, 49, 51, 52, 54, 55, 58, 60, 61, 71, 78, 79, 83, 101-104, 109
REWARD 15, 81, 82
REWARDS....13, 81, 82, 96
RICH......44, 69, 81, 91, 93-95, 122, 123
RICH MAN....44, 69, 91, 93-95, 123
RIDICULE 120
RIDICULED......... 25
RIDING 114
RIGHT....11, 29, 83, 86, 89, 124, 143
RIGHT HAND ... 124, 143
RIGHTEOUSNESS... 11, 20, 130, 132, 135, 140
RIPPLE 105
RISEN 119, 125
RIVER 105
ROBE 121
ROCK 83
ROWS 105

165

RULE 24, 49
RULERS 113
RUN 55, 57, 70, 80, 129
SACRIFICE ... 22, 63, 82, 99
SACRIFICED 67
SAFETY 136
SAINTS .. 20, 47, 49, 56, 69, 75
SALVATION 5, 7, 13, 110, 125, 129, 139, 141
SAND 52
SATAN 5, 23, 40, 41-44, 47, 49, 51, 52, 54, 72-74, 80, 101, 109, 132, 140, 143, 144
SAVE 56, 62, 109, 111, 114, 119, 121, 135, 137, 139, 140
SAVED 5, 9, 22, 26, 34, 35, 54, 60, 62, 64, 66, 81, 88, 90, 97, 98, 102, 106, 111, 122, 125, 128, 136, 137, 141, 143, 144, 146, 184
SAVIOUR 9, 35, 55, 90, 95, 98,
109, 118, 121, 136, 141
SAW 46, 47, 49, 75, 101
SCARES 26
SCOURGE 144
SCOURGED 120
SCOURGING 120
SCRAPS 93
SCRIPTURE 5, 7, 9, 15, 32, 64, 91, 133, 173
SEA 101
SEALED 45
SEASHORE 52
SECOND 25, 45, 60, 83, 95, 131
SECOND DEATH . 60, 83, 131
SEED 109, 131
SEEK 90, 135
SELF ... 5, 18, 23, 41, 86, 135, 140
SELF GRATIFICATION 86
SELF-MADE 135
SEPARATED 12, 37, 75, 131
SERVANT 9, 20, 56, 57, 116
SERVANTS ... 20, 21, 30, 31, 35, 58

INDEX

SERVE......5, 19, 26, 31, 35, 44, 105, 132
SERVICE........9, 20, 22, 23, 26, 28, 29, 35, 36, 63, 184
SETTLED 71, 106
SEVERE 85, 87
SHALT.............. 136
SHAME.......31, 119, 121
SHEKINAH GLORY 103
SHINING............ 14
SHIP 90
SHORT.....5, 24, 26, 114, 129
SHORTCOMINGS.29
SIDE..75, 105, 119, 121
SIGHT.14, 105, 129
SILVER 69, 116
SIMPLE 141
SIN...7, 11, 18, 19, 51, 72, 74, 83, 85, 87, 92, 101, 129-135, 138-141, 143, 144, 146
SINNER..69, 85, 91, 111, 129

SINNERS...56, 109, 123, 129, 130, 137, 139
SINS........9, 13, 19, 36, 44, 50, 58, 62, 66, 67, 69, 74, 79, 92, 110, 111, 118, 122, 134, 135, 137, 138, 140
SIX DAYS 72, 74
SLAVE 117
SLEEPING......... 106
SLIPPERY SLOPE 109
SLUMBERETH 39
SMELL 68
SMOKE 61
SMOKING 144
SOBER.. 80, 81, 133
SOBERING...... 9, 88
SO-CALLED......109, 135
SODOM............... 87
SON......40, 57, 84, 97, 104, 109, 111, 113, 114, 119, 121, 127, 131, 137, 139, 141, 144
SONS OF GOD....28, 127
SORROW 102

SOUL.....29, 32, 57, 62, 80, 133
SOULS....21, 53, 60, 81, 105, 119, 124
SOVEREIGNTY.. 111
SOWED 131
SOWETH 84
SOWING 62, 131
SPARED 39
SPECTACULAR.... 97
SPEEDING......... 129
SPIRIT 28, 141
SPIRITUAL. 23, 146
SPOILS 125
SPOKE............... 131
SPRING............. 105
STAGE 37
STALKING 80
STALKS 133
STAND 81
STANDARD........ 24, 129, 130
STARS................. 97
STEAL 19
STERN............... 106
STOP.. 80, 102, 138
STRAYING......... 146
STRIPPED 121
STRIVING 135
STRONGER 21
STUDY......9, 10, 19, 21, 26, 33, 34, 37, 110
STUMBLING 85

SUCCESS 99
SUFFER..15, 23, 35, 58, 59, 118, 119
SUFFICIENT. 30, 103
SUN............. 97, 103
SURELY 38, 39, 117
SURFACE 105
SWIFTLY 38
SWIM 104
SYMBOLIC 15
SYNAGOGUE....... 42
SYSTEM 23, 83
TABERNACLE 102
TABLE....... 7, 91, 93
TAKERS 56
TAKING 139
TALLAHASSEE, FLORIDA......... 104
TARES 131, 132
TASKS 31
TEACHES......23, 58, 72, 84, 129
TEACHING 10, 28
TEETH................. 29
TELEPHONES 25
TEMPLE 103
TEMPORARY 142
TEMPTATION.... 134
TEMPTED 74, 131
TESTIFIED...89, 97, 125, 128
TESTIMONY......132

INDEX

THE GREAT WHITE THRONE JUDGMENT..... 12, 37, 40, 44, 45, 49, 53, 55, 57, 60, 64-66, 119, 144
THIELMAN J. VAN BRAGHT 24
THIEVES 122
THINGS..13, 18, 31, 35, 58, 68, 71, 90, 98, 100, 102, 136, 140, 141
THINK....11, 21, 26, 27, 36, 51, 81, 85, 93, 102, 129, 141, 146
THINKING........ 129
THIRTY 116
THOMAS........... 119
THORNS........... 121
THOUGHT......13, 15, 36, 95, 120
THOUGHTS....... ..10, 130, 134
THOUSAND YEARS 49, 54
THOUSANDS 25, 80
THREE.....40-42, 56, 97, 125
THREE PERSONS. 40, 41
THRONE....... 7, 105

TODAY.....5, 13, 24, 25, 38, 45, 67, 93, 97, 109, 129, 146
TOMB........119, 124, 125, 127
TOMORROW. 66, 146
TONGUE.......45, 57, 69, 94
TORMENT....12, 45, 59, 61, 67, 69, 75, 79, 94, 96, 131
TORMENTED....... 37, 44, 52, 54, 78
TORMENTS...69, 78, 81
TORTURE.....25, 69, 121
TOTALLY .. 136, 139
TOUCH . 44, 94, 139
TOWARD......23, 41, 68, 138
TOWER............. 105
TRANSFORMED... 23
TRANSGRESSION 18, 129
TRANSGRESSIONS 118
TRANSLATED..... 67, 75, 117
TRAPPED.......... 132
TREASURES........ 99

169

TREATABLE 135
TREATED 143
TREMBLE............ 53
TRIALS.............. 142
TRIBULATION ... 43, 47, 51
TRINITY.............. 41
TRIUMPHANTLY......
......................114
TRIUNE 56
TROUBLED 97
TRUCK............... 100
TRUE..89, 106, 139, 146
TRUST...37, 50, 53, 54, 66, 93, 127, 136, 139, 141, 146
TRUSTING.......... 54, 135, 139
TRUTH......5, 11, 26, 40, 67, 83, 87, 88, 90, 94, 99, 117, 129, 131, 140
TRUTHS........37, 38, 127
TURN..........49, 120, 132, 136
TURNING.. .... 109, 135, 138, 139
TWO MASTERS ... 44
UNACCEPTABLE 22, 63

UNBELIEVERS 42
UNDER 143, 184
UNDERSTANDING...
.... 88, 135, 142
UNEARNED 139
UNIFORM 59
UNIMAGINABLE 25, 102
UNION..............141
UNIT 85, 110
UNITE..................60
UNITED STATES
.... 105, 184
UNIVERSE 71, 90
UNJUST 118
UNMERITED 21, 139
UNPROFITABLE .21, 30, 31
UNRELENTING....61
UNRIGHTEOUSNESS
......................129
UNSAVED 58, 60
UNSPEAKABLE....62
UPPER HELL 94
VARYING............58
VEHICLES...........25
VERDICT......55, 58, 136
VICIOUS.............13
VICTORY 109
VIGILANT....80, 81, 133
VILE 120
VILLAGE.............90

INDEX

VINDICATED 13
VIOLATE 130
VIRGIN 111, 184
VISIBLE 14, 71, 144
WAGES .83, 99, 117
WAIT 143
WAKE UP 65
WAKULLA SPRINGS 104
WALK 94, 104
WALKING 145
WALL 138
WAR 47
WARN 64, 65
WARNED 73, 84, 133
WARNING .. 21, 106
WATCH .5, 106, 107
WATER....26, 78, 93, 94, 105
WEEKS 110
WET 44, 69
WHEAT 131
WHIP 120
WHIPPED 118
WHITE 7, 90, 95
WHOSOEVER..... .24, 68, 130
WHY 32, 34, 53, 58, 62, 64, 72, 94, 96, 128, 144
WICKED 13, 55, 122, 132, 135
WICKEDNESS ... 129
WIDOW 82
WIDOWS 85
WILDERNESS ... 102
WIN 144
WITHDRAW 140
WITNESS 19, 89, 95
WOMAN 111, 130
WONDER 15, 25, 97
WONDERFUL ... 102, 109
WONDERS 133
WORD 5, 11, 14, 18, 19, 22, 26-28, 30, 31, 34, 35, 41, 67, 70, 71, 75, 99, 109, 117, 142
WORDS 9, 14, 15, 18, 34, 56, 67, 68, 106, 119, 139
WORKMAN 33
WORKS ...13-15, 58, 60, 81, 83, 133
WORLD ..19, 23, 40, 50, 89, 93, 95, 102, 105, 131, 133, 139, 142
WORLDWIDE 103
WORM 120
WORMS 105
WORSHIP ... 31, 104
WOUNDED 118

WRATH .. 19, 52, 86
WRITTEN.....29, 32, 64, 104
WRITTEN WORD 29
YEAR................... 62
YEARS...10, 27, 29, 38, 42, 45, 46, 110, 119, 120, 122, 184
YIELD 20, 22
YOURSELF....68, 80, 100

LIST OF SCRIPTURE REFERENCES

BOOKS	PAGE
Genesis 1:1	72
Genesis 1:27	72
Genesis 2:8	72
Genesis 3:1	74
Genesis 3:3	74
Genesis 3:6	74
Numbers 16:28-33	75
Deuteronomy 5:1	32
Deuteronomy 7:12	32
Deuteronomy 26:16	33
Deuteronomy 32:4	83
Joshua 24:15	66
Psalm 2:1-3	113
Psalm 11:5	11
Psalm 16:9-10	77
Psalm 22:6-8	120
Psalm 41:9	115
Psalm 68:18	124
Psalm 86:11-13	94

ARE YOU READY?

Psalm 119:89	71
Psalm 126:5	62
Proverbs 1:31	11
Isaiah 7:14	111
Isaiah 14:9	75
Isaiah 14:12-15	73
Isaiah 53:4-6	117
Isaiah 53:9	122
Isaiah 59:1-2	137
Isaiah 64:4	100
Jeremiah 17:9	135
Ezekiel 3:17-21	64
Ezekiel 22:31	11
Ezekiel 26:20	75
Ezekiel 33:7-8	65
Daniel 9:24-25	110
Daniel 12:11	42
Micah 5:2	112
Zechariah 9:9	114
Zechariah 11:12	116
Zechariah 12:10	118
Matthew 1:18-23	111
Matthew 2:1	112

SCRIPTURE REFERENCES

Reference	Page
Matthew 3:16-17	40
Matthew 5:6	113
Matthew 5:21-22	69
Matthew 5:28	130
Matthew 5:41	30
Matthew 6:19-20	99
Matthew 7:21-23	11
Matthew 7:23	61
Matthew 8:12	61
Matthew 11:20-24	87
Matthew 12:38-40	77
Matthew 13:24-25	131
Matthew 13:28	131
Matthew 13:30	131
Matthew 13:37-40	131
Matthew 16:27	81
Matthew 21:1-9	114
Matthew 22:37	54
Matthew 23:13-14	85
Matthew 25:31	51
Matthew 25:41, 46	12
Matthew 26:14-16	117
Matthew 26:24-25	116

Matthew 27:26-31	122
Matthew 27:38	122
Matthew 27:57-60	123
Matthew 28:18-20	34
Matthew 28:19	62
Mark 7:20-23	134
Mark 9:44, 48	134
Mark 12:41-44	82
Mark 13:31-37	106
Luke 5:32	135
Luke 9:23	24
Luke 9:26	25
Luke 12:47-48	88
Luke 13:3	49
Luke 14:23	35
Luke 14:27	24
Luke 16:13	44
Luke 16:19-31	44, 69, 75, 91
Luke 16:27-28	95
Luke 17:7-10	30
Luke 23:43	77
Luke 24:1-8	125
John 1:9	89

SCRIPTURE REFERENCES

John 3:3	27
John 3:16	49
John 3:18	137
John 5:22	26
John 6:27	49
John 6:47	49
John 12:47	13
John 14:1	43, 44
John 14:1-3	44, 97
John 14:15	32, 63, 141
John 14:15-17	141
John 14:21	63
John 15:8	63
John 15:20	35
John 19:10-11	84
John 19:38-42	123
John 20:27-28	118
Acts 1:3	127
Acts 1:9-11	128
Acts 4:25-27	113
Romans 2:12-15	89
Romans 3:23	129
Romans 5:8	137

Romans 6:13	20
Romans 6:16	20
Romans 6:18	20
Romans 8:14	28
Romans 10:9-10	136
Romans 10:9-12	140
Romans 10:13	141
Romans 12:1-2	21, 63
1 Corinthians 2:9	100
1 Corinthians 3:11-15	13
1 Corinthians 6:9-10	65
1 Corinthians 10:13	134
1 Corinthians 10:21	42
1 Corinthians 11:30	144
1 Corinthians 15:6	125
2 Corinthians 4:3-4	38
2 Corinthians 5:8	98
2 Corinthians 5:10	12
2 Corinthians 5:17	19
2 Corinthians 5:20	99
2 Corinthians 6:2	146
2 Corinthians 13:5	96
Galatians 4:4-7	127

SCRIPTURE REFERENCES

Reference	Page
Galatians 4:7	141
Galatians 5:19-21	49
Ephesians 1:7	19
Ephesians 2:2	23
Ephesians 2:8-9	53
Ephesians 4:8	74
Philippians 2:5-11	56
Philippians 3:20-21	98
Philippians 4:7	141
Colossians 1:18	41
Colossians 3:23-25	18
1 Thessalonians 4:13-17	51
1 Thessalonians 5:17	33
1 Timothy 4:1	39
2 Timothy 2:15	33
Hebrews 5:12-14	27
Hebrews 12:5-11	144
James 1:13-15	131
James 1:19-20	86
James 1:22	28
James 2:10	130
James 2:19	53
James 3:1	86

1 Peter 2:2	27
1 Peter 2:24	53
1 Peter 3:18	117
1 Peter 5:8	80, 133
2 Peter 3:9	38, 138
2 Peter 2:1-4	37
2 Peter 2:3	38
2 Peter 2:4	39
2 Peter 3:9	138
1 John 1:4-7	145
1 John 1:8, 10	129
1 John 1:9	135
1 John 2:1-2	143
1 John 3:4	18
Revelation 1:18	71
Revelation 3:9	42
Revelation 4:10-11	31
Revelation 9:3-11	16
Revelation 13:15	15
Revelation 14:9-11	78
Revelation 19:11-21	46
Revelation 2:9	42
Revelation 20:1	43, 49

SCRIPTURE REFERENCES

Revelation 20:10	15, 43, 49
Revelation 20:11-15	55
Revelation 20:12	58
Revelation 20:14	60
Revelation 20:2	49, 52
Revelation 20:7-10	54
Revelation 21:1-3	101
Revelation 21:7	102
Revelation 21:16	103
Revelation 22:1-4	104
Revelation 21:22-27	103

ABOUT THE AUTHOR

LEO & ELSIE LAVINKA

    LEO ROBERT LAVINKA WAS BORN IN 1934. HE WAS RAISED IN MONTICELLO, FLORIDA, BUT NOT IN A CHRISTIAN HOME. AFTER HIGH SCHOOL AND ONE TOUR IN THE AIR FORCE, HE ATTENDED FLORIDA STATE UNIVERSITY BEFORE TRANSFERRING TO THE UNIVERSITY OF FLORIDA WHERE HE GRADUATED WITH A BACHELOR OF CIVIL ENGINEERING DEGREE. HE WORKED FOR

THE U.S. ARMY CORPS OF ENGINEERS IN THE JACKSONVILLE, FLORIDA, DISTRICT BEFORE TRANSFERRING TO THE DIVISION OFFICE IN ATLANTA, GEORGIA IN 1969. HE BEGAN HIS CAREER IN CONSTRUCTION AND HAD OPPORTUNITY TO PARTICIPATE IN MANY DIFFERENT MILITARY AND CIVIL ENGINEERING PROJECTS IN THE SOUTHEAST UNITED STATES, PUERTO RICO, U.S. VIRGIN ISLANDS, PANAMA CANAL ZONE, AND SOMETIMES IN OTHER CENTRAL AND SOUTH AMERICA COUNTRIES.

IN 1973 HE TRANSFERRED FROM CONSTRUCTION TO EMERGENCY MANAGEMENT WHERE HE WAS RESPONSIBLE FOR PLANNING, COORDINATING, TRAINING, AND EXECUTION OF THE CORPS' MISSIONS TO SUPPORT THE MILITARY, AND NATURAL DISASTERS RECOVERY EFFORTS. HIS RESPONSIBILITY EXPANDED TO THE MIDDLE EAST BEFORE AND DURING DESERT SHIELD, DESERT STORM, AND KUWAIT RECOVERY. HE IS THE RECIPIENT OF SEVERAL AWARDS FOR HIS SERVICE AND RETIRED IN 1999 AFTER 39 YEARS OF SERVICE TO THE U.S. GOVERNMENT.

HE WAS SAVED IN 1969 WHILE ATTENDING FORREST HILLS BAPTIST CHURCH IN DECATUR, GEORGIA, UNDER THE MINISTRY OF DR. CURTIS HUTSON AND THE WITNESSING OF A COWORKER. HE WAS ORDAINED AS A DEACON BY PASTOR HUTSON IN 1970. HE ALSO SERVED AS A

SCRIPTURE REFERENCES

DEACON AT CORINTH BAPTIST CHURCH, LOGANVILLE, GEORGIA UNDER PASTOR DON RICHARDS; RETURN BAPTIST CHURCH, DEMOREST, GEORGIA UNDER PASTOR WALTER BURRELL; AND IS CURRENTLY A DEACON, TREASURER, AND SECRETARY AT ZION HILL BAPTIST CHURCH, CLEVELAND, GEORGIA UNDER PASTOR NATHAN NIX, (ALL INDEPENDENT, FUNDAMENTAL BAPTIST CHURCHES).

HE HAS TAUGHT SUNDAY SCHOOL FROM ELEMENTARY TO ADULTS IN SEVERAL CHURCHES AND SERVED IN THE BUS MINISTRY AT FORREST HILLS BAPTIST CHURCH. HE HAS ALSO BEEN A JANITOR, YARD KEEPER, AND A TEACHER AT A SATELLITE CHURCH. HE HAS BEEN ACTIVE IN VISITATION PROGRAMS FROM 1970 TO THE PRESENT.

www.ingramcontent.com/pod-product-compliance
Lightning Source LLC
LaVergne TN
LVHW051557070426
835507LV00021B/2633